TIKI COCKTAILS

13-Digit ISBN: 978-1-64643-373-5
10-Digit ISBN: 1-64643-373-4

This book may be ordered by mail from the publisher. Please include $5.99 for postage and handling. Please support your local bookseller first!

Books published by Cider Mill Press Book Publishers are available at special discounts for bulk purchases in the United States by corporations, institutions, and other organizations. For more information, please contact the publisher.

Cider Mill Press Book Publishers
"Where good books are ready for press"
PO Box 454
12 Spring Street
Kennebunkport, Maine 04046

Visit us online!
cidermillpress.com

Typography: Ayr Tropika Island Interlock, Ayr Tropika Island Script Casual, VVDS Halau, Filmotype Wand, House-A-Rama Kingpin, Aktiv Grotesk,

Pages 12, 16–17, 19, 22–23, 32–33, 38, 42, 45, 46, 64–65, 76, 86–87, 92–93, 118–119, 172–173, 180–181, 182, and 193 used under official license from Shutterstock.com. Pages 4-5, 6 used under Creative Commons 2.0 license. All other photos courtesy of Cider Mill Press.

Printed in China

1 2 3 4 5 6 7 8 9 0

First Edition

TIKI
COCKTAILS

OVER 125 FLAVOR-PACKED TROPICAL COCKTAILS

CIDER MILL PRESS

BOOK PUBLISHERS
KENNEBUNKPORT, MAINE

CONTENTS

INTRODUCTION

CHANCES ARE, one of your first cocktails was a streamlined take on tiki, pairing the sweet, flavorful character of rum with a brightly flavored juice and/or a tropically inclined ingredient such as cream of coconut.

In truth, these pared-down versions are a far cry from what you'll find in this book and in the world's best bars, where talented practitioners of tiki fashion concoctions of astonishing depth and complexity. But they do manage to capture some of what is so appealing about tiki cocktails, which manage to be delicious, accessible, refreshing, and refined at the same time.

While you're no doubt intrigued by cocktails that feature all of these characteristics, you're also probably wondering how tiki managed to gather all of them together.

Tiki is a strange amalgamation of craft, imagination, escapism, and cultural appropriation. Looking at it from certain vantage points, it seems to be little more than an exceptionally effective marketing strategy. From others, tiki veers dangerously close to tacky. From another point of view, it is a craft that rewards precision and daring, one that without a doubt produces some of the best cocktails in the world today. In truth, tiki is a heady mix of all of these things, and, while we are primarily concerned with the mixological aspects in this book, a true appreciation can only come through taking a close look at the elements that fostered the enigmatic essence of these cocktails.

The tiki conversation can only start in one place, with one man: Don the Beachcomber. Born Ernest Gantt in 1907, Gantt ripped through an inheritance galivanting around the world and drinking in everything from the South Pacific to the Caribbean. Eventually, Gantt's funds ran out, and he found himself in Los Angeles, making ends meet with a series of odd jobs—including one that involved him lending the artifacts he'd gathered during his travels to movie studios looking to give their sets a bit of authenticity. By 1933, Gantt had saved enough to open his own place, and turned a small room that had been a tailor shop into Don's Beachcomber, a charmingly run-down rum shack in the middle of Hollywood. Adorned with his numerous treasures and featuring cocktails that pushed the flavors Gantt had fallen in love with during his prodigal years, the bar was an instant hit.

Gantt, who eventually leaned fully into his construction and changed his name to Donn Beach (the bar's name was also changed, to Don the Beachcomber), was certainly a marketing wizard. But he was also a daring mixologist who not only had impeccable taste, but an artist's willingness to tinker and revise until the final product was just right. He discovered that by blending rums, he could give a cocktail added complexity and a strong backbone. By incorporating spices, fresh juices, and sweeteners, he could transport his guests a world away from the hustle and bustle of the city outside the door. While the tiki palate continues to grow, it was Beach's love for citrus, pineapple, passion fruit, maple syrup, grenadine, allspice liqueur, peach brandy, coffee, Angostura, and, of course, rum that provided its foundation.

The exotic building blocks of Donn's cocktails went into unmarked bottles, coded in a manner that only he knew—not even the Beachcomber's bartenders knew exactly what was in the drinks people revered them for crafting. Unfortunately for Beach, and fortunately for the rest of us, his security measures proved not to be enough. In the 1930s, Don the Beachcomber had a customer who was so eager and so inquisitive about what was happening that the employees branded him "The Rope Hanger." That watchful regular was Vic Bergeron, an Oakland restaurateur, and while Vic's vigilance quickly got him bounced, he took Donn's blueprint and used it to make over his own restaurant. The rest is history. Vic used everything he'd soaked up to expand Beach's vision, adding spirits such as gin, pisco, and tequila to the mix, and also incorporating the beguiling French syrup orgeat (it's pronounced "ore-zha"), an innovation that led to the creation of the Mai Tai, what many believe to be the ultimate tiki cocktail. But Bergeron did more than just expand what could be considered tiki—he expanded its reach. Ever open the menu at a Chinese-American restaurant and be charmed and confused by the page of cocktails bearing an exotic look and occasionally ridiculous names? That is another piece of Vic's legacy, as he was the first to understand that this hybrid cuisine was the perfect partner for tropical-leaning cocktails, and put his theory into practice at a new restaurant in San Francisco—Trader Vic's. This restaurant was quickly the toast of the Bay Area, and his establishments soon spread around the country, an expansion aided in large part by the Polynesian craze that had seized the United States.

For a while tiki's momentum seemed unstoppable, but eventually, the craft that Beach and Vic built their empires upon was lost, and the cocktails carrying the tiki torch stopped seeking balance and began to emphasize the strong and sugary elements, and eschewed fresh fruit and juices for prefabricated blends that were closer to what a car mechanic would employ than a mixologist. This decline, combined with an increasingly thoughtful culture that was uncomfortable with what tiki had co-opted from island peoples and cultures, pushed tiki to the dusty corners of cocktail culture.

And there tiki stayed, a kitschy symbol of a bygone era, its appeal apparent to just a handful of true believers. Eventually, one of those believers, Jeff "Beachbum" Berry, would devote himself to cracking Beach's codes, talking with old bartenders who had come of age in tiki's heyday. In 1997, Berry compiled the early results of this work in *Beachbum Berry's Grog Log*. The book did well enough to bring Berry's project to the attention of Jennifer Santiago, the daughter of a former Beachcomber bartender. Jennifer handed Berry her father's notebook, and though it was in Donn's arcane codes (featuring bespoke and inscrutable ingredients such as Donn's Mix and Spices #4), Berry persisted, poring over this tome for years. The books that have resulted from this study, including *Intoxica* and *Beachbum Berry's Sippin' Safari*, returned tiki to respectability in cocktail culture, and inspired Martin Cate and others to honor and expand on Donn Beach's vision.

While this book can only capture a small bit of what tiki spans, the hope is that it inspires others to forge their own path through tiki's twisted maze. And if not, at the very least, it is certain to provide endless enjoyment and refreshment.

THE CLASSICS

A collection of those cocktails that powered tiki's rise, and retain enough magic to fuel its recent renaissance.

PLANTER'S PUNCH

"ONE OF SOUR, two of sweet, three of strong, four of weak," is the jingle known throughout the Caribbean that leads to the creation of a delicious punch. This particular serve is the best of what resulted.

2 oz. Appleton Estate Reserve Blend rum

½ oz. Grenadine (see page 256)

¼ oz. Demerara Syrup (see page 256)

¼ oz. St. Elizabeth Allspice Dram

½ oz. fresh lime juice

2 dashes of Angostura Bitters

1. Place all of the ingredients, except for the bitters, in a cocktail shaker, fill it two-thirds of the way with ice, and shake vigorously until chilled.

2. Fill the Collins glass with ice and strain the cocktail over it.

3. Top the cocktail with the bitters, garnish it with the edible orchid, and enjoy.

HALEKULANI

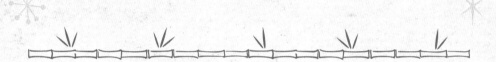

MAKE SURE THERE'S ALWAYS A BOTTLE of Baker's bourbon around the house. It's got the kick you want in a cocktail, and the smoothness you want when sipping bourbon neat.

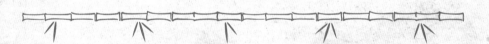

1½ oz. Baker's bourbon

½ oz. Demerara Syrup (see page 256)

1 bar spoon of Grenadine (see page 256)

½ oz. pineapple juice

½ oz. fresh orange juice

½ oz. fresh lemon juice

Dash of Angostura Bitters

1. Chill the coupe in the freezer.

2. Place all of the ingredients in a cocktail shaker, fill it two-thirds of the way with ice, and shake vigorously until chilled.

3. Strain the cocktail into the chilled coupe.

4. Garnish the cocktail with the orange slice or dehydrated pineapple chunk and enjoy.

ZOMBIE

IN THE SPIRITS WORLD, only absinthe is more notorious than this cocktail, which many tiki aficionados cite as Donn Beach's very best formula.

1½ oz. Appleton Estate Signature Blend rum

1½ oz. Smith & Cross rum

1 oz. 151-proof rum

6 drops of absinthe

½ oz. falernum

1 bar spoon of Grenadine (see page 256)

½ oz. Donn's Mix (see page 257)

¾ oz. fresh lime juice

Dash of Angostura Bitters

1. Place all of the ingredients in a cocktail shaker, fill it two-thirds of the way with ice, and shake vigorously until chilled.

2. Fill the Zombie mug with crushed ice and strain the cocktail over it.

3. Garnish the cocktail with the fresh mint and lime shell and enjoy.

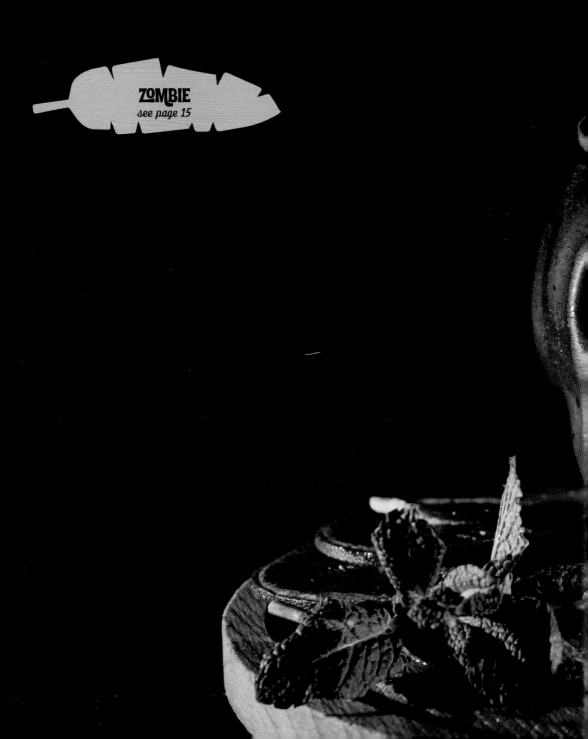

ZOMBIE
see page 15

THREE DOTS AND A DASH

THE NUMBER OF CHERRIES to use for garnish is rarely specified in this book, but here they help carry out the message in Morse code that inspired the name of the drink.

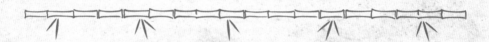

1½ oz. rhum agricole

½ oz. El Dorado 3-Year rum

¼ oz. St. Elizabeth Allspice Dram

½ oz. falernum

½ oz. Honey Syrup (see page 269)

½ oz. fresh orange juice

½ oz. fresh lime juice

1. Place all of the ingredients in a cocktail shaker, fill it two-thirds of the way with ice, and shake vigorously until chilled.

2. Fill the Collins glass with ice and strain the cocktail over it.

3. Thread the cherries on a skewer.

4. Garnish the cocktail with the cherries and pineapple leaves and enjoy.

DOCTOR FUNK

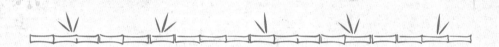

ADD AS MUCH, or as little, Pernod as you want here, as it is the most up-front component in the drink. If you decide to trim the amount, add a little bit more bitters.

½ oz. fresh lemon juice

¼ oz. Grenadine
(see page 256)

½ oz. fresh lime juice

½ oz. Demerara Syrup
(see page 256)

Dash of Pernod

Dash of Angostura Bitters

2¼ oz. Hamilton Jamaica
Black rum

1 oz. seltzer

1. Place all of the ingredients in a cocktail shaker, fill it two-thirds of the way with ice, and shake vigorously until chilled.

2. Fill the Collins glass with crushed ice and strain the cocktail over it.

3. Garnish the cocktail with the pineapple leaves and enjoy.

GLASSWARE: Collins glass
GARNISH: Pineapple wedge, Luxardo maraschino cherries,
lime wedge, fresh mint

SUFFERING BASTARD

THE RARE CLASSIC that didn't come to us from either Don the Beachcomber or Trader Vic. Instead, this was created by Joe Scialom, a dashing bartender in Cairo during World War II, and it is said to have supplied Allied forces with much grit in their effort to push back the Germans.

1 oz. Cognac

1 oz. dry gin

⅔ oz. Lime Cordial (see page 257)

⅓ oz. fresh lime juice

3 dashes of Angostura Bitters

3⅓ oz. ginger beer

1. Place all of the ingredients, except for the ginger beer, in a cocktail shaker, fill it two-thirds of the way with ice, and shake vigorously until chilled.

2. Fill the Collins glass with crushed ice and strain the cocktail over it.

3. Top the cocktail with the ginger beer.

4. Garnish the cocktail with the pineapple wedge, Luxardo maraschino cherries, lime wedge, and fresh mint and enjoy.

SUFFERING BASTARD
see page 21

MAI TAI

THERE IS SOME DEBATE over where and when the Mai Tai was created, with various factions arguing for both Don the Beachcomber and Trader Vic as the progenitor. This version favors the latter, but only because the origin story is better. According to legend, Vic whipped it up and served it to two friends visiting from Tahiti. One of them, Carrie Guild, according to Trader Vic's lore, took a sip and replied, "Mai tai—roa ae." Translated from Tahitian, that means, "Out of this world—the best."

2 oz. Appleton Estate Reserve Blend rum

¾ oz. curaçao

½ oz. Orgeat (see page 258)

½ oz. fresh lime juice (reserve spent lime shell for garnish)

¼ oz. Rock Candy Syrup (see page 259)

1. Place all of the ingredients, except for the garnishes, in a cocktail shaker, fill it two-thirds of the way with crushed ice, and shake vigorously until chilled.

2. Pour the contents of the shaker into the Mai Tai glass, garnish with the fresh mint and reserved lime shell, and enjoy.

HURRICANE

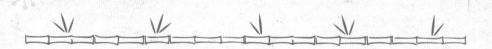

A FAR MORE REFINED VERSION than what you will find at the establishment renowned for popularizing the drink, Pat O'Brien's in New Orleans. Don't let your guard down, however—this is just as potent as the elixir you'll encounter on Bourbon Street.

1 oz. Hamilton Jamaica Black rum

1 oz. Appleton Estate Reserve Blend rum

1¼ oz. Passion Fruit Blend (see page 258)

¼ oz. fresh lemon juice

Dash of Peychaud's Bitters

1. Place all of the ingredients in a cocktail shaker, fill it two-thirds of the way with crushed ice, and shake vigorously for three times as long as usual.

2. Pour the contents of the shaker into the Hurricane glass, garnish with the lemon wheel, and enjoy.

CARIBBEAN MILK PUNCH

A SILKY MIX of classic and contemporary makes this a timeless cocktail.

1 oz. Vanilla Syrup
(see page 259)

1 oz. Smith & Cross rum

½ oz. bourbon

1 oz. heavy cream

1. Place all of the ingredients in a cocktail shaker, fill it two-thirds of the way with ice, and shake vigorously until chilled.

2. Fill the tumbler with ice and strain the cocktail over it.

3. Garnish the cocktail with the freshly grated nutmeg and enjoy.

MISSIONARY'S DOWNFALL

IF YOU LIVE OUTSIDE of a big city, a steady supply of apricot liqueur—whether your preference be for Rothman & Winter or Giffard—can be tough to arrange. Should you run out but be craving this drink, peach schnapps is a workable substitute.

1 oz. Diplomático Añejo rum

½ oz. apricot liqueur

½ oz. Honey & Cinnamon Syrup (see page 260)

½ oz. grapefruit juice

1½ oz. pineapple juice

½ oz. fresh lime juice

10 to 15 fresh mint leaves, plus more for garnish

1. Place all of the ingredients in a cocktail shaker, add crushed ice, and flash mix with a hand blender.

2. Pour the contents of the shaker into the Hurricane glass, garnish with the orange wheel and fresh mint, and enjoy.

MARY PICKFORD

CREATED IN CUBA to honor the legendary actress and founder of United Artists while she was shooting a film on the island, this cocktail is a snapshot of a much different time, in so many ways.

½ oz. Banks 5 Island rum

1½ oz. pineapple juice

1 teaspoon Grenadine (see page 256)

6 drops of Luxardo maraschino liqueur

1. Chill a coupe in the freezer.

2. Place all of the ingredients in a cocktail shaker, fill it two-thirds of the way with ice, and shake vigorously until chilled.

3. Strain the cocktail into the chilled coupe, skewer the cherries on a toothpick, garnish the cocktail with them, and enjoy.

MARY PICKFORD
see page 31

NAVY GROG

A DRINK SO ENTICING that even the buttoned-up Richard Nixon could not resist it—legend holds that the disgraced president used to sneak into Trader Vic's in the wee hours of the morning and down a few Navy Grogs while unburdening himself to the bartender.

1 oz. Appleton Estate
Signature Blend rum

1 oz. Smith & Cross rum

1 oz. El Dorado 5 Year rum

1 oz. Demerara Syrup
(see page 256)

¾ oz. fresh lime juice

¾ oz. fresh grapefruit juice

¼ oz. St. Elizabeth Allspice
Dram

1. Place all of the ingredients in a cocktail shaker, fill it two-thirds of the way with ice, and shake vigorously until chilled.

2. Fill the tumbler with crushed ice and strain the cocktail over it.

3. Garnish the cocktail with the lime shell and enjoy.

JET PILOT

THIS IS AN EVOLUTION of the Test Pilot, which Donn Beach created around 1941. Eventually, Beach turned to his old standby, cinnamon, and a surefire classic was born.

1 oz. Smith & Cross rum

¾ oz. Don Q Añejo rum

6 dashes of Pernod

¾ oz. 151-proof rum

½ oz. falernum

½ oz. Cinnamon Syrup (see page 260)

½ oz. white grapefruit juice

½ oz. fresh lime juice

Dash of Angostura Bitters

1. Place all of the ingredients in a cocktail shaker, fill it two-thirds of the way with ice, and shake vigorously until chilled.

2. Fill the rocks glass with pebble ice and strain the cocktail over it.

3. Garnish the cocktail with the Luxardo maraschino cherry, pineapple leaves, and fresh mint and enjoy.

PAINKILLER

THE NAME SAYS IT ALL—this doesn't just alleviate what's bothering you, it removes it entirely from this realm.

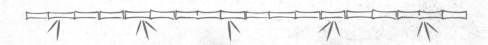

2½ oz. Hamilton Guyana 86 rum

1 oz. cream of coconut

1 oz. orange juice

4 oz. pineapple juice

1. Place all of the ingredients in a cocktail shaker, fill it two-thirds of the way with crushed ice, and shake vigorously until chilled.

2. Pour the contents of the shaker into the tiki mug, garnish with the orange slice, cinnamon stick, and freshly grated nutmeg, and enjoy.

SCORPION BOWL

AS THIS IS TRADITIONALLY a group affair, the recipe here will serve four people. But it can also easily work as a stand-alone cocktail if you cut back on the amounts, but maintain the same ratios.

2 oz. fresh lime juice

4 oz. fresh orange juice

1 oz. Demerara Syrup
(see page 256)

2 oz. Orgeat (see page 258)

1 oz. Grenadine
(see page 256)

2 oz. brandy

4 oz. London Dry gin

4 oz. Diplomático Reserva
rum

1. Place all of the ingredients in a cocktail shaker and pour it into another cocktail shaker or mixing glass to combine.

2. Divide the cocktail between the two vessels, add crushed ice to each, and flash mix with a hand blender.

3. Pour the contents of the vessels into the ceramic scorpion bowl, garnish with the Flaming Lime Shell, and enjoy.

FOG CUTTER

VIC CAME UP with this drink, but Donn's decision to swap pisco in for the Cognac is an insight that can't be overlooked, adding a freshness and depth that come through clear as day.

1½ oz. fresh lemon juice

1½ oz. fresh orange juice

½ oz. Orgeat (see page 258)

1 oz. pisco

½ oz. London Dry gin

2 oz. Brugal 1888 rum

½ oz. oloroso sherry

1. Place all of the ingredients, except for the sherry, in a cocktail shaker, fill it two-thirds of the way with ice, and shake vigorously until chilled.

2. Fill the tiki mug with crushed ice and strain the cocktail over it.

3. Float the sherry on top of the cocktail, pouring it over the back of a spoon.

4. Garnish the cocktail with the fresh mint and enjoy.

GLASSWARE: Coupe
GARNISH: Dehydrated pineapple slice

BLUE HAWAIIAN

IF YOU NEED something cooler, add the ingredients to a blender along with ½ cup of ice and puree for 5 seconds. Pour it into a Hurricane glass and enjoy.

¾ oz. vodka

¾ oz. Pusser's rum

½ oz. blue curaçao

3 oz. pineapple juice

1 oz. Sweet & Sour
(see page 261)

1. Place all of the ingredients in a cocktail shaker, fill it two-thirds of the way with ice, and shake vigorously until chilled.

2. Fill the coupe with crushed ice and strain the cocktail over it.

3. Garnish the cocktail with the dehydrated pineapple slice and enjoy.

JUNGLE BIRD

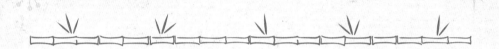

SERVED AS THE welcome drink at the Hilton Kuala Lumpur upon its opening in 1973, this cocktail took a while to enter the tiki canon, but has now become a fixture—at bars of all kinds.

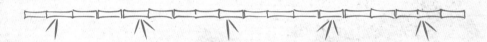

2 oz. Smith & Cross rum

¾ oz. Campari

1½ oz. pineapple juice

½ oz. fresh lime juice

1. Place all of the ingredients in a cocktail shaker, fill it two-thirds of the way with ice, and shake vigorously until chilled.

2. Fill the rocks glass with ice and strain the cocktail over it.

3. Garnish the cocktail with the pineapple wedge and enjoy.

SINGAPORE SLING

THIS IS ONE OF THE OLDEST tiki drinks, with its invention coming sometime in the early twentieth century. Much of the debate surrounding the Singapore Sling centers around what should make up the cherry component, so if the Heering isn't quite doing it for you, experiment with kirsch, cherry brandy, or even some syrup from a jar of Luxardo maraschino cherries.

1½ oz. London Dry gin

½ oz. Cherry Heering

¼ oz. Benedictine

½ oz. fresh lemon juice

¼ oz. Demerara Syrup (see page 256)

Dash of Angostura Bitters

Dash of orange bitters

1. Place all of the ingredients in a cocktail shaker, fill it two-thirds of the way with ice, and shake until chilled.

2. Fill the Collins glass with ice and strain the cocktail over it.

3. Garnish the cocktail with the edible flowers and enjoy.

❀ TIKI COCKTAILS

RIFFS & REFINEMENTS

With its relatively complex formulas and beautifully balanced flavors, tiki has long been a fertile ground for experimentation by mixologists, providing plenty of opportunities to employ their unique perspectives and put a twist on the classics.

IF YOU LIKE PIÑA COLADAS

THE SECRET RUM BLEND is a mix of overproof, Jamaican, and Venezuelan rums. The exact recipe is a highly guarded industry secret, so tinker until you find a mix that's to your liking!

2 oz. secret rum blend

2 oz. fresh pineapple juice

1 oz. cream of coconut

¼ oz. fresh lemon juice

3 coffee beans

½ oz. Lustau Pedro Ximénez Sherry, to float

1. Fill the Hurricane glass with ice.

2. Build the cocktail in the glass, adding all of the ingredients, except for the sherry, to the glass in the order that they are listed.

3. Float the sherry on top of the cocktail, pouring it over the back of a spoon.

4. Garnish the cocktail with the Luxardo maraschino cherry, tiki umbrella, and fresh mint.

PERFECT STORM

TART, SWEET, and spicy, this elevated Hurricane is a whirlwind of flavors.

1 oz. Plantation O.F.T.D. rum

1 oz. Banks 5 Island Rum

¾ oz. pineapple juice

½ oz. fresh lime juice

½ oz. Rhubarb Syrup
(see page 262)

½ oz. Honey & Ginger Syrup
(see page 262)

½ oz. Grenadine
(see page 256)

Chocolate-Infused Don Q 151
(see page 262), to float

1. Add all of the ingredients into a mixing glass filled with ice, except for the Chocolate-Infused Don Q 151, and use the swizzle method to combine: place a swizzle stick between your hands, lower the swizzle stick into the drink, and quickly rub your palms together to rotate the stick as you move it up and down in the drink. When frost begins to form on the outside of the glass, the drink is ready.

2. Fill the Collins glass with pebble ice and strain the cocktail over it.

3. Float the infused rum on top of the cocktail, pouring it over the back of a spoon.

4. Garnish the cocktail with the pineapple leaf and cherry and enjoy.

COGNAC KONG

THE ORIGINAL KING KONG is sweet, and that cloying nature was part of what contributed to tiki's downfall in the '70s. By using Cognac instead of coconut rum, the cocktail becomes suitable for the modern palate.

1½ oz. Cognac

½ oz. banana liqueur

½ oz. falernum

1 oz. fresh lemon juice

3 oz. pineapple juice

1. Place all of the ingredients in a cocktail shaker, fill it two-thirds of the way with ice, and shake vigorously until chilled.

2. Fill the tiki mug or Collins glass with crushed ice and strain the cocktail over it.

3. Garnish the cocktail with the Grenadine, cinnamon, pineapple wedge, and Banana Dolphin and enjoy.

THE TOUGH GET GOING

PURISTS WILL SAY that the rum float throws the Mai Tai out of whack, but topping it with the balanced but indulgent flavor of Santa Teresa rum proves that the evolution is a good one.

1½ oz. Royal Standard Dry Rum

½ oz. fresh orange juice

½ oz. Orgeat (see page 258)

½ oz. curaçao

¼ oz. fresh lime juice

½ oz. Santa Teresa 1796 rum

1. Place all of the ingredients, except for the Santa Teresa rum, in a cocktail shaker, fill it two-thirds of the way with ice, and shake vigorously until chilled.

2. Fill the large tumbler with crushed ice and strain the cocktail over it.

3. Float the Santa Teresa rum on top of the cocktail, pouring it over the back of a spoon.

4. Garnish with the strip of orange peel and enjoy.

GLASSWARE: Tiki mug

GARNISH: Dehydrated lemon wheel, fresh mint, dried chile pepper, freshly grated allspice

THE LAST BASTARD

THE CONCLUSION OF THE SAGA started by the Suffering Bastard cocktail.

⅔ oz. London Dry gin

⅔ oz. umeshu

⅔ oz. Bigallet China-China Amer liqueur

⅔ oz. fresh orange juice

2 bar spoons of fresh lime juice

2 dashes of Dale DeGroff's Pimento Aromatic Bitters

1. Add all of the ingredients, except for the bitters, to the tiki mug.

2. Insert a swizzle stick into the mixture and fill the glass halfway with crushed ice.

3. Use the swizzle method to mix the cocktail: place a swizzle stick between your hands, lower the swizzle stick into the drink, and quickly rub your palms together to rotate the stick as you move it up and down in the drink. When frost begins to form on the outside of the tiki mug, the drink is ready.

4. Top the glass with more crushed ice and the bitters, garnish with the dehydrated lemon wheel, fresh mint, dried chile pepper, and allspice, and enjoy.

MAISON ABSINTHE COLADA

THE PIÑA COLADA is not quite tiki royalty, but the inventive twists its popularity have fostered do give it an impressive lineage.

1 oz. absinthe

½ oz. Martinique rhum agricole

1 bar spoon of crème de menthe

1 oz. pineapple juice

½ oz. fresh lemon juice

1 oz. Coconut Syrup (see page 263)

1. Place all of the ingredients in a cocktail shaker, fill it two-thirds of the way with ice, and shake vigorously until chilled.

2. Fill the Hurricane glass with ice and strain the cocktail over it.

3. Garnish the cocktail with the fresh mint and enjoy.

FALLEN ANGEL

THIS DRINK IS A TWIST on the Missionary's Downfall, and starts from a much higher place.

3 springs of fresh mint

½ oz. fresh lime juice

1 oz. pineapple juice

½ oz. Honey Syrup
(see page 269)

½ oz. banana liqueur

1½ oz. Ron Zacapa 23 rum

1. Place the fresh mint in a cocktail shaker and gently muddle it. Add the remaining ingredients and three ice cubes to the shaker and whip shake vigorously until chilled.

2. Fill the wineglass with crushed ice and strain the cocktail over it.

3. Garnish the cocktail with the fresh mint and Banana Dolphin and enjoy.

PART OF TIKI'S ALLURE is its emphasis on aesthetics, mixing kitsch, spirituality, shabby chic, and theatrics in a manner one can't help but be charmed by. This visual awareness leaves plenty of space for creative and eye-catching garnishes that both complement the elements present in a cocktail and communicate tiki's fun and free-spirited nature, such as the Flaming Lime Shell (see page 114). Though this is a go-to tiki garnish, we understand that fire and alcohol aren't for everyone. If that's the case, here are three more alluring garnishes to turn to when you're trying to turn someone on to tiki.

THE BANANA DOLPHIN is a dramatic tour de force that can adorn any tiki drink. To make it, cut the bottom fifth off of a banana. Slice off ¼ inch of the stem tip of the banana, and slice through the stem to make the dolphin's mouth. Make a slit on the bottom of the banana, about 1 inch in from where you made your initial cut. You want to make sure this slit goes to the equator of the banana, as this will help the garnish stay on the rim of the glass. Insert one clove on each side of the banana, above the dolphin's mouth, affix the garnish to the glass, and enjoy.

THE COBRA HEAD shows that there's no reason for anyone to fear snakes. To form this garnish, run a channel knife along the perimeter of a lime until you have a 4-inch strip of peel. Cut a separate lime into wedges. Remove the pulp from one of the wedges. This wedge will be used to form the head of the snake. Fold the snake's head in half and make two small holes in the top. Insert a whole clove into each hole, to form the eyes. Use an orchid petal to make the snake's tongue. Fasten the head to the 4-inch strip of peel with a cocktail pick, affix the garnish to the glass, and enjoy.

THE PINEAPPLE FIREBIRD is another garnish that lends a bit of theater to a tiki drink, particularly those where you're using the hollowed-out pineapple as a drinking vessel. To make the Firebird, cut off the top of the pineapple about an inch beyond the base of the leaves. Vertically segment the pineapple top into 4 to 6 sections (depending on size of fruit) so that each section has a bit of pineapple flesh and a plume of leaves. Cut a slit at a 45-degree angle from the inner flesh toward the peel. Insert a toothpick vertically through the smaller segment of flesh. Put a cherry on the toothpick and position the garnish so that the stem hangs over the beverage, giving the illusion that the "bird" is drinking from the glass.

GAMORA'S ZOMBIE

THE BESPOKE MIX adds a warm spicy note that bolsters the complexity of the rums.

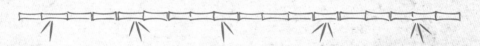

1 oz. The Real McCoy 5 Year rum

1 oz. Appleton Estate Signature Blend rum

¼ oz. Marlo's Mix (see page 263)

¾ oz. Passion Fruit Syrup (see page 263)

¾ oz. fresh ruby red grapefruit juice

¾ oz. fresh lime juice

¼ oz. absinthe

1 oz. Hamilton Guyana 151 rum

1. Place all of the ingredients, except for the 151 rum, in a blender and puree until combined.

2. Fill the Zombie mug with pebble ice and pour the cocktail over it.

3. Float the 151 rum on top of the cocktail, pouring it over the back of a spoon.

4. Garnish with the fresh mint, Luxardo maraschino cherry, lime wheel, and tiki umbrella and enjoy.

MY KINDA GAL

AN ADVANCED orgeat keys this twist on the Mai Tai.

¾ oz. Banana & Cashew Orgeat (see page 264)

1½ oz. Hamilton Guyana 86 rum

½ oz. Mandarine Napoléon liqueur

1 oz. fresh lime juice

½ oz. Ron Zacapa 23 rum, to float

1. Place all of the ingredients, except for the Ron Zacapa rum, in a cocktail shaker, fill it two-thirds of the way with ice, and shake vigorously until chilled.

2. Fill the rocks glass with ice and strain the cocktail over it.

3. Float the Ron Zacapa rum on top of the drink, pouring it slowly over the back of a spoon.

4. Garnish with the fresh mint, orange slice, and maraschino cherry and enjoy.

CAMPARI COLADA

CAMPARI'S BITTERNESS, along with its subtle citrusy spice, make it a seemingly unusual spirit to put forth in a Piña Colada. In reality, it's perfect.

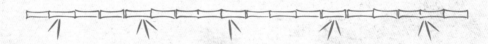

3 oz. fresh pineapple juice

1 oz. cream of coconut

1 oz. heavy cream

2 oz. Campari

1. Place all of the ingredients in a cocktail shaker with no ice and dry shake for 10 seconds.

2. Fill the tiki mug with crushed ice, pour the cocktail over it, and then use the swizzle method to mix the drink: place a swizzle stick between your hands, lower the swizzle stick into the drink, and quickly rub your palms together to rotate the stick as you move it up and down in the drink. When frost begins to form on the outside of the tiki mug, the drink is ready.

3. Garnish the cocktail with the orange slice and Luxardo maraschino cherry and enjoy.

WHISKEY VIC

TIKI BY WAY of Appalachia.

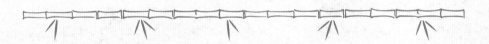

1½ oz. moonshine

½ oz. curaçao

½ oz. Orgeat (see page 258)

½ oz. fresh lime juice

¼ oz. fresh lemon juice

1. Place all of the ingredients in a cocktail shaker, fill it two-thirds of the way with ice, and shake vigorously until chilled.

2. Fill the Collins glass with ice and strain the cocktail over it.

3. Garnish the cocktail with the Luxardo maraschino cherry, orange wheel, and lemon wedges and enjoy.

THE PAMPAS

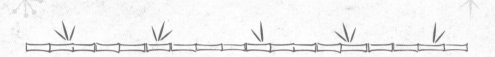

RHUM AGRICOLE'S SIGNATURE grassy note is enough to transform the Mai Tai.

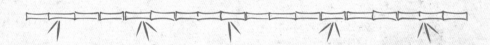

1½ oz. Appleton Estate Signature Blend rum

½ oz. rhum agricole

½ oz. Demerara Syrup (see page 256)

½ oz. Orgeat (see page 258)

½ oz. curaçao

1. Place all of the ingredients in a cocktail shaker, fill it two-thirds of the way with ice, and shake vigorously until chilled.

2. Fill the Mai Tai glass with ice and strain the cocktail over it.

3. Garnish the cocktail with the lime shell and fresh mint and enjoy.

GLASSWARE: Tiki mug
GARNISH: Fresh mint, strawberry, dehydrated orange wheel

ZOMBIE KILLER

THERE'S NO HARD-AND-FAST RULE on what overproof rums you go with here, but a Jamaica-centric one—utilizing Wray & Nephew and Smith & Cross—is a good place to start.

1¾ oz. overproof rum blend

¾ oz. Pink Zombie Mix (see page 264)

½ oz. fresh lime juice

½ oz. fresh pineapple juice

½ oz. cream of coconut

Dash of absinthe

1. Place the ingredients in a cocktail shaker and add 5 oz. of crushed ice.

2. Flash mix with a hand blender and then pour the contents of the shaker into the tiki mug.

3. Garnish the cocktail with the fresh mint, strawberry, and dehydrated orange wheel and enjoy.

ALL TAI'D UP

THIS MAI TAI VARIANT relies heavily on the Maple & Pecan Falernum. It does take a while to make it, but it's well worth it.

1 banana leaf

2 oz. bourbon

1 oz. Maple & Pecan Falernum (see page 265)

½ oz. fresh orange juice

½ oz. fresh lime juice

½ oz. curaçao

1. Trim the banana leaf into a rectangle and place it on the bottom of the rocks glass. Fill the glass with pebble ice.

2. Combine the remaining ingredients in a cocktail shaker, fill it two-thirds of the way with ice, and shake vigorously until chilled.

3. Strain the cocktail into the glass, garnish with the lime wheel, edible orchid, and fresh mint, and enjoy.

EL PAJARO

20

EL PÁJARO

THIS RIFF ON the Jungle Bird, where the tart Hibiscus Syrup balances out the sweet pineapple juice, is named after a card in the Mexican bingo game, Lotería.

1 oz. fresh orange juice

¼ oz. fresh lime juice

1 oz. fresh pineapple juice

½ oz. Hibiscus Syrup
(see page 264)

¼ oz. mezcal

¾ oz. Campari

1 oz. Plantation 3 Stars rum

1. Place the orange juice in a blender and pulse to "fluff" the juice. Set the orange juice aside.

2. Build the cocktail in the Collins glass, adding the remaining ingredients in the order they are listed. Fill the glass with crushed ice, leaving a ½ inch of space for the orange juice.

3. Slowly pour the fluffed orange juice over the crushed ice.

4. Garnish the cocktail with the Brûléed Pineapple and fresh mint and enjoy.

BRÛLÉED PINEAPPLE: Simply place some sugar in a dish, roll a pineapple wedge in the sugar until it is coated, and then use a kitchen torch to brulée the pineapple.

PINUP ZOMBIE

THE GARNISHES may seem involved, but they build the bridges between the numerous flavors here.

1 oz. Bacardí Añejo Cuatro rum

1 oz. Pusser's Gunpowder Proof rum

2 teaspoons Santa Teresa 1796 rum

½ oz. Quaglia Liquore di Ciliegia cherry liqueur

2 teaspoons Quaglia Liquore al Pino Mugo pine liqueur

2 teaspoons falernum

1 oz. Passion Fruit Syrup (see page 263)

¾ oz. fresh pink grapefruit juice

½ oz. fresh lime juice

1. Place all of the ingredients in a cocktail shaker, fill it two-thirds of the way with ice, and shake vigorously until chilled.

2. Fill your chosen mug with crushed ice and strain the cocktail over it.

3. Add more crushed ice and place the passion fruit husk and pineapple leaves on top.

4. Add a spoonful of passion fruit and a generous pinch of coconut sugar to the cocktail.

5. Combine 2 teaspoons each of rum and absinthe, pour the mixture into the passion fruit husk, and light it with a long match. Sprinkle cinnamon over the flames and enjoy the cocktail.

JUNGLE BABBLER

A CONSIDERED BLEND of rums and the tart passion fruit display the Jungle Bird with all its plumage.

½ teaspoon Demerara Syrup (see page 256)

¼ oz. Grenadine (see page 256)

1 bar spoon of Passion Fruit Syrup (see page 263)

½ oz. fresh lime juice

¾ oz. pineapple juice

¼ oz. Hamilton Guyana 151 rum

½ oz. Cognac

¾ oz. Appleton Estate Reserve Blend rum

¾ oz. El Dorado 3 Year rum

¼ oz. Campari

4 dashes of Cruzan Black Strap rum

Dash of absinthe

1. Place all of the ingredients in a cocktail shaker, fill it two-thirds of the way with ice, and shake vigorously until chilled.

2. Fill the Collins glass with crushed ice and strain the cocktail over it.

3. Garnish with the pineapple wedge and pineapple leaves.

GLASSWARE: Rocks glass
GARNISH: Fresh mint, tiki umbrella

MAI WAY OR THE HIGHWAY

THE POTENT HERBAL FLAVORS of Underberg mean that this twist won't be for everyone, but those who abide will be enjoying themselves too much to worry about it.

1 oz. Smith & Cross rum

1 oz. Aperol

1 oz. fresh lime juice

½ oz. Orgeat (see page 258)

½ oz. curaçao

1 miniature bottle of Underberg

1. Place all of the ingredients, except for the Underberg, in a cocktail shaker, fill it two-thirds of the way with ice, and shake vigorously until chilled.

2. Fill the rocks glass with crushed ice and strain the cocktail over it.

3. Carefully flip the bottle of Underberg into the cocktail so it is upside down. Garnish the cocktail with the fresh mint and tiki umbrella and enjoy.

EL CUCO

A REFRESHING, ice-cold take on the Navy Grog. A tip for this and any other tiki drink jammed with crushed ice: use a chopstick to bore a hole through the ice so you can access the drink with a straw.

1 oz. Appleton Estate Signature Blend rum

½ oz. Hamilton Guyana 86 rum

½ oz. Caña Brava 7 Year rum

½ oz. El Dorado 3 Year rum

¾ oz. fresh lime juice

¾ oz. grapefruit juice

¾ oz. Honey & Ginger Syrup (see page 262)

Seltzer, to top

1. Place all of the ingredients, except for the seltzer, in a cocktail shaker, fill it two-thirds of the way with ice, and shake vigorously until chilled.

2. Fill the rocks glass with crushed ice and strain the cocktail over it.

3. Top the cocktail with the seltzer, garnish it with the lime wedge and fresh mint, and enjoy.

TIKI COCKTAILS

THE NEXT GENERATION

Tiki is no different than any other craft—
there are practitioners who are focused on
honoring the tradition, and those who want
to follow the direction these classic forms
point. This chapter collects cocktails that
retain tiki's focus on rum, but look to expand
what that spirit is capable of.

A BRIEF OVERVIEW OF RUM

Though tiki drinks that do not have rum in them are becoming increasingly common, as the last chapter of the book shows, a desire to get into tiki means that one is also going to become a connoisseur of rum.

As it is easily the most diverse spirit on Earth, the process of gaining this knowledge is a fun one. But it also can be overwhelming, with offerings from more than 60 countries available to sample.

To start, rum is known for its sweetness, and, considering that it is made by distilling sugarcane or sugarcane byproducts, there's no getting away from this aspect of its flavor profile. The industry rose from the sticky dregs of colonialism, which flourished in the Caribbean thanks to the free labor provided by slavery. Rum is the result of yeast being added to the molasses that is a by-product of boiling the juice from harvested sugarcane. This "wash" is then allowed to ferment for anywhere from 24 hours to 2 weeks, and then distilled. The fermentation process affects rum's flavor in two ways. The length of the fermentation period will have considerable impact, with more aromatic and flavorful substances developing the longer the fermentation is allowed to proceed. The second major influence is the type of yeast used. Many distillers have developed their own distinct strains over the years and are highly protective of them—in fact, Bacardí is so concerned about the possible corruption of the yeast used to power their global empire that they store some of the original in a climate-controlled vault in Switzerland. A few Jamaican producers utilize a method similar to the sourdough starter that has become all the rage in bread baking. Kept in "dunder pits," wood-lined pits hidden in the ground, these wild yeasts are fed by leftover wash, eventually producing the funk Jamaican rums are known and loved for.

Once the wash is made, it has to be distilled to produce rum. The pot still is the oldest of the methods used to distill rum, and it is essentially a large kettle where the wash is brought to a boil, with any vapors condensed and collected. Another pass through the pot still will then bring the spirit to proof, and then the rum will be rested in stainless steel tanks or oak barrels so that the bold flavors present when the rum comes out of the still can mellow. For centuries, the pot still was the only option available to distillers, but with the Industrial Revolution came the advent of the column still, an innovation that proved to be a huge leap forward in terms of production and efficiency. A column still requires less wash and less energy to produce spirits, and it also can be fed continuously with wash, as opposed to the batches which must be added and then removed from the pot still. Another advantage of the column still is the higher-proof and lighter-bodied spirit it produces, a style that has a much broader appeal. But, for all of those advantages, the column still cannot touch the pot in terms of creating the various aromas and flavors that appeal to the craftsman and the connoisseur. To solve this problem, rum producers have followed in the footsteps of the Scottish, who have been using a combination of pot and column distillates to create blended Scotch whisky since the nineteenth century. Grabbing the best of both approaches, the spirits are then blended and aged or aged separately before being combined, resulting in rums that are smoother on the palate and more complex, despite not being aged for as long as they typically would have to be to achieve these measures.

People assume that any clear rum is not aged, though that is not the case for all but a few products on the market. In most white or clear rums, the color has been removed via charcoal filtration. This misapprehension regarding clear rums also feeds the belief that all of the golden-hued rums on the shelf get that color from the barrel. That may well be the case, but a 's color can also come from a distiller adding caramel coloring, a practice used to trick the uninitiated into thinking complexity and depth will be there, when in reality they aren't. As for black rums, they are typically unaged or very briefly aged blended rums that receive their dark shade from the addition of caramel and/or molasses. In this category, a consideration of color is actually helpful, because it defines the category.

In light of the complications that can result from using color as a guide, some will rely on the age statement featured on the spirit's label. But this can also imply a wide range of possibilities. In some countries, like Barbados, Jamaica, and Guyana, the age statement will be the youngest rum featured in the blend. In other countries, such as those which use the solera-style method of aging, the age statement will reflect the oldest spirit present. And, on occasion, the rum will forgo a precise mention of age and employ terms that imply extended stints in a barrel, like "añejo" or "XO," but are not guided by any strict guidelines.

In this book, blended rums that have been lightly aged (1 to 4 years), such as Appleton Estate's Funky Reserve Blend, or El Dorado's 3 Year offering, do a majority of the lifting, and rums in this age range have been rested long enough to let the nature of the spirit come through, but not long enough to take on too much influence from the barrel, beyond color. But there are more than a few instances where a more mature rum, aged from 5 to 14 years, is called for. For those familiar with the higher price tags that extended aging can come with, rest assured—these aged rums, which are also wonderful for sipping neat, carry a much lower price tag than similarly aged Scotches or bourbons. For the devotee of blended rums, Venezuela's Diplomático and El Dorado are the best aged options, while Ron Zacapa 23 and Flor de Caña are wonderful options produced via the column still.

In your travels through the world of tiki, you will also come across rhum agricole and caçhaca. The former is made from sugarcane juice instead of molasses, and, since it is not fermented before being distilled, it tends to by drier and more vegetal than its close cousin. Caçhaca is often referred to as "Brazilian rum," as it is the South American nation's preferred spirit. Like rum, it is fermented, but, as with rhum, sugarcane juice is the raw material. This results in a grassier, rawer spirit that is more inclined to being affected by elements like terroir and the type of wood used to age it than other rums.

Of course, any trip to the rum section at a liquor store is going to meet with a numbered of flavored rums. In short, the serious tiki practitioner should avoid them at all costs, and take matters into their own hands, whether it be making their own spiced rum (see page 274), or simply incorporating the flavor they want—coconut, mango, passion fruit—into the cocktail as they mix it.

GLASSWARE: Double rocks glass

GARNISH: Freshly grated nutmeg

NACIONAL

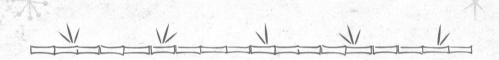

SUZE'S BITTERSWEET FLAVOR allows all of the other elements here to shine.

¼ oz. banana liqueur

¼ oz. Suze

¼ oz. apricot liqueur

¾ oz. fresh lime juice

½ oz. pineapple juice

½ oz. Yuzu Syrup
(see page 266)

¼ oz. Banana Syrup
(see page 267)

2 oz. Banks 5 Island rum

1. Place all of the ingredients in a cocktail shaker, fill it two-thirds of the way with ice, and shake vigorously until chilled.

2. Fill the double rocks glass with ice and strain the cocktail over it.

3. Garnish the cocktail with the freshly grated nutmeg and enjoy.

WHAT'S UP, DOC?

TIKI COCKTAILS UNDERSTAND one thing better than any other category of drinks: "You drink with your eyes first."

2 oz. Black Currant–Infused Rum (see page 266)

¾ oz. fresh lemon juice

¾ oz. carrot juice

½ oz. orange juice

¼ oz. Ginger Syrup (see page 273)

¼ oz. maple syrup

Dash of Dale DeGroff's Pimento Aromatic Bitters

1. Place all of the ingredients in a cocktail shaker, fill it two-thirds of the way with ice, and shake vigorously until chilled.

2. Fill the footed pilsner glass with crushed ice and strain the cocktail over it.

3. Garnish the cocktail with the carrot greens and enjoy.

GLASSWARE: Tumbler
GARNISH: Flaming Lime Shell (see page 114),
grapefruit slice, lime wheel, edible orchid

BELLA SoCo

THE BOUQUET OF FRUIT SLICES and orchid acts as both a garnish and a barrier for the guest to sip behind while allowing the flame to seemingly burn forever.

1½ oz. cachaça

½ oz. El Dorado 15 Year rum

¼ oz. Hamilton Guyana
151 rum

1½ oz. Donn's Mix
(see page 257)

¾ oz. fresh lime juice

¼ oz. Demerara Syrup
(see page 256)

Dash of Angostura Bitters

1. Place all of the ingredients in a cocktail shaker, add 2 ice cubes, and whip shake vigorously until chilled.

2. Fill the tumbler with crushed ice and strain the cocktail over it.

3. Garnish the cocktail with the Flaming Lime Shell, grapefruit slice, lime wheel, and edible orchid and enjoy.

ISLAND TIME

DON'T BE FOOLED by the garnish—this one doesn't bite.

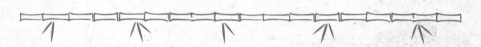

½ oz. fresh lemon juice

¼ oz. Passion Fruit Syrup (see page 263)

½ oz. Orgeat (see page 258)

½ oz. falernum

½ oz. 151-proof rum

1 oz. Diplomático Añejo rum

1 oz. Appleton Estate Signature Blend rum

Dash of Angostura bitters

2 dashes of absinthe

1. Place all of the ingredients in a cocktail shaker, fill it two-thirds of the way with ice, and shake vigorously until chilled.

2. Fill the rocks glass with crushed ice and strain the cocktail over it.

3. Garnish the cocktail with the Cobra Head and enjoy.

CURIOUS GEORGE

USING FIREBALL gives this drink a sense of mischievous fun.

1½ oz. cachaça

¾ oz. banana liqueur

½ oz. fresh lemon juice

½ oz. Fireball cinnamon whisky

1. Place all of the ingredients in a cocktail shaker, add 2 ice cubes, and whip shake vigorously until chilled.

2. Fill the rocks glass with crushed ice and strain the cocktail over it.

3. Garnish the cocktail with the cinnamon and dehydrated banana chips and enjoy.

TOURIST TRAP

AN EXPRESSION of Jamaica's rich rum history mixed with the tropical flavors and spices native to the island.

2 oz. Coconut Rum Blend
(see page 266)

1 oz. fresh lime juice

1 oz. Tiki Mix (see page 267)

¼ oz. Orgeat (see page 258)

2 dashes of Bittercube
Jamaican No. 1 Bitters

1. Build the cocktail in the tiki mug, adding all of the ingredients, except for the bitters, to the mug in the order they are listed.

2. Fill the glass with crushed ice and use the swizzle method to mix the drink: place a swizzle stick between your hands, lower it into the drink, and quickly rub your palms together to rotate the stick as you move it up and down in the drink. When frost begins to form on the outside of the tiki mug, the drink is ready.

3. Top the cocktail with the bitters, garnish it with the fresh mint and slice of mango, and enjoy.

VERY HUNGRY MANZANILLA

PARAPHRASED FROM THE famed children's book by Eric Carle, *The Very Hungry Caterpillar*, this very grown-up drink has plenty of depth, belying the green coloring. Also, these might be the best garnishes in the entire book.

1¼ oz. Plantation 3 Stars rum

½ oz. amontillado sherry

¾ oz. fresh lime juice

½ oz. Sage & Mint Agave (see page 268)

Seltzer, to top

1. Place all of the ingredients, except for the seltzer, in a cocktail shaker, fill it two-thirds of the way with ice, and shake vigorously until chilled.

2. Fill the Collins glass with ice and double-strain the cocktail over it.

3. Top the cocktail with the seltzer, garnish it with the perforated sprig of fresh mint and candy caterpillar, and enjoy.

KANJI IN THE EVENING

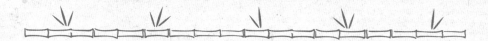

IF YOU HAVE ONE, use a smoke gun to add a fragrant cherrywood aroma to the mix—the smoke also looks mighty classy.

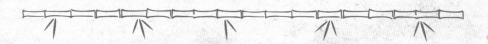

1 oz. Appleton Estate Signature Blend rum

¾ oz. Ron Zacapa 23 rum

1¾ teaspoons Yellow Chartreuse

½ oz. Aperol

½ oz. Pink Pepper & Pomegranate Syrup (see page 268)

¾ oz. fresh lime juice

1. Place all of the ingredients in a cocktail shaker, fill it two-thirds of the way with ice, and shake vigorously until chilled.

2. Place an ice sphere in the rocks glass and double-strain the cocktail over it.

3. If desired, use a smoke gun filled with cherry-wood chips to smoke the drink. Don't leave it running too long: 10 to 15 seconds is about right.

GOOD FORTUNE

THE ACIDITY OF THE ORANGES, yuzu, and lime blends elegantly with the smoky sweetness of the Zacapa rum, and the touch of heat from the Vanilla & Chile Syrup really rounds off the drink.

1⅜ oz. Ron Zacapa 23 rum

¾ oz. umeshu

2 teaspoons orange marmalade

1 oz. fresh lime juice

½ oz. Vanilla & Chile Syrup (see page 269)

1. Chill the cocktail glass in the freezer.

2. Place all of the ingredients in a cocktail shaker, fill it two-thirds of the way with ice, and shake vigorously until chilled.

3. Double-strain the cocktail into the chilled cocktail glass, garnish with a Torched Orange Twist, and enjoy.

TORCHED ORANGE TWIST: Cut a rounded slice of orange peel, at least 1 inch in diameter. It's not a problem if it gets some of the pith; a thick peel is fine. Hold the strip of orange peel about 2 inches above a lit match for a few seconds. Twist and squeeze the peel over the lit match, while holding it above the cocktail.

RUM BA BA

NAMED AFTER THE French cake, this cocktail is not as sweet as you'd think, considering the ingredients. Think of this as part of an adult version of milk and cookies.

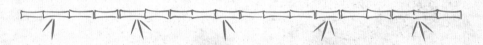

1½ oz. Appleton Estate Reserve Blend rum

1½ oz. heavy cream

1 oz. Orgeat (see page 258)

½ oz. fresh lemon juice

1¼ oz. passion fruit puree

2 dashes of Peychaud's Bitters

1. Place all of the ingredients in a cocktail shaker, fill it two-thirds of the way with ice, and shake vigorously until chilled.

2. Fill the rocks glass with ice and double-strain the cocktail over it.

3. Garnish with the passion fruit slice and fresh mint and enjoy.

OPEN SÉSAME

TAHINI IS AN UNUSUAL cocktail ingredient. That makes it perfect to incorporate into a tiki cocktail, where its rich, nutty flavor can find its way.

1½ oz. Flor de Caña 12 Year rum

1 oz. añejo tequila

¼ oz. crème de cacao

½ oz. chocolate syrup

1 oz. heavy cream

½ oz. coconut milk

½ oz. tahini paste

1. Place all of the ingredients in a cocktail shaker, except for ½ oz. of the heavy cream, fill it two-thirds of the way with ice, and shake vigorously until chilled.

2. Fill the rocks glass with crushed ice and strain the cocktail over it.

3. Remove the ice from the shaker, add the remaining heavy cream, and shake until it is frothy.

4. Pour the frothy cream on top of the cocktail, garnish it with the toasted coconut and harissa powder or za'atar, and enjoy.

FEISTy MEISTER

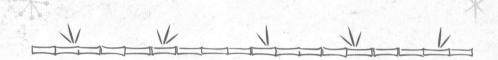

THIS DRINK requires flame—and a bit of caution.

½ oz. Appleton Estate Signature Blend rum

½ oz. Plantation 5 Year rum

1 oz. Jägermeister

½ oz. fresh orange juice

½ oz. fresh lime juice

½ oz. Passion Fruit Syrup (see page 263)

½ oz. Orgeat (see page 258)

1. Place all of the ingredients in a cocktail shaker, add crushed ice, and flash mix with a hand blender.

2. Pour the contents of the shaker into the Collins glass.

3. Squeeze the juice out of the lime shell and then fill it with 151-proof rum. Set it atop the cocktail. Using a long match, light the rum on fire and sprinkle cinnamon over the flame to make it spark. Enjoy the show while you wait until the flame burns out.

HAITIAN DIVORCE

RHUM BARBANCOURT 5 STAR is typically reserved for sipping, but its sweet, slightly oaky flavor is needed to stand up to the other ingredients here.

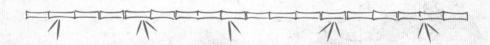

1½ oz. Rhum Barbancourt 5 Star

¾ oz. mezcal

½ oz. Pedro Ximénez sherry

2 dashes of Angostura Bitters

1. Fill the rocks glass with large ice cubes. Add the ingredients to the glass and stir until chilled.

2. Garnish with the orange and lime twists and enjoy.

BEACHCOMBER

A STRAIGHTFORWARD, refreshing homage to the man who started it all, Donn Beach.

1½ oz. Mount Gay Eclipse rum

¾ oz. curaçao

½ oz. fresh lime juice

1 bar spoon of Luxardo maraschino liqueur

½ bar spoon of Demerara Syrup (see page 256)

1. Chill the coupe in the freezer.

2. Place all of the ingredients in a cocktail shaker, fill it two-thirds of the way with ice, and shake vigorously until chilled.

3. Strain the cocktail into the chilled coupe, garnish with the lime wedge, and enjoy.

SHARK'S BITE

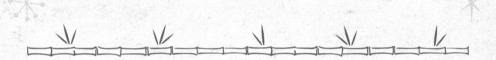

STRAIGHTFORWARD, strong, and with surprising depth, the Shark's Bite shows how much promise tiki has in the modern mixology world.

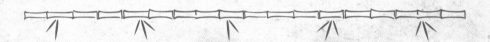

2 oz. Wray & Nephew rum

3 oz. fresh orange juice

½ oz. fresh lime juice

¾ oz. Grenadine
(see page 256)

1. Place the rum, orange juice, and lime juice in a cocktail shaker, add crushed ice, and flash mix with a hand blender.

2. Pour the contents of the shaker into the Collins glass. Float the Grenadine on top of the cocktail, pouring it over the back of a spoon, and enjoy.

GLASSWARE: Coupe
GARNISH: Lime wheel

AMBASSADOR PUNSCH

PUNSCH, A STYLE OF liqueur popular in Sweden and other Nordic countries, used to be an important part of many cocktails, but largely disappeared because of Prohibition. This cocktail will go a long way toward putting it back in the spotlight.

1 oz. Plantation 5 Year rum

1 oz. punsch

½ oz. Demerara Syrup
(see page 256)

½ oz. fresh lime juice

6 drops of Bittermens
'Elemakule Tiki Bitters

1. Chill the coupe in the freezer.

2. Place all of the ingredients in a cocktail shaker, fill it two-thirds of the way with ice, and shake vigorously until chilled.

3. Strain the cocktail into the chilled coupe, garnish with the lime wheel, and enjoy.

JOJO RABBIT

DON'T TOSS your used pineapple shells once you've removed the fruit from them. Instead, store them in the freezer and break them out whenever you need an extra bit of escape.

1½ oz. Plantation Pineapple rum

½ oz. apricot liqueur

1 oz. pineapple juice

½ oz. fresh lime juice

¼ oz. Demerara Syrup (see page 256)

4 dashes of Peychaud's Bitters

1. Place all of the ingredients, except for the bitters, in a cocktail shaker, fill it two-thirds of the way with ice, and shake vigorously until chilled.

2. Double-strain the cocktail into the pineapple and top with the bitters.

3. Garnish the cocktail with the pineapple leaves, orange slices, fresh mint, and tiki umbrella and enjoy.

ISLAND HOPPER

FRESHLY PRESSED HAWAIIAN sugarcane produces some fantastic rum, and fortunately, there is a small crop of young, exciting distilleries that have opened up in the Islands, like Oahu's Kō Hana Distillers.

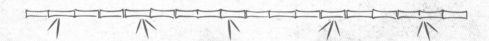

1 oz. Don Q Cristal rum

½ oz. Kō Hana Kea Agricole

½ oz. Hibiscus Syrup
(see page 264)

½ oz. fresh lemon juice

¾ oz. pineapple juice

2 oz. ginger beer

1. Place all of the ingredients, except for the ginger beer, in a cocktail shaker, fill it two-thirds of the way with ice, and shake vigorously until chilled.

2. Place the ginger beer in the Collins glass, strain the cocktail into the glass, and fill it with crushed ice.

3. Garnish the cocktail with the pineapple leaves and dehydrated lime wheel and enjoy.

SLOE SUNSET

WHEN SHOPPING for pomegranate liqueur, PAMA is the one and only choice. Although you could just substitute Grenadine (see page 256) and funk this up with another rum.

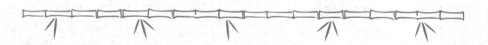

1 oz. Hibiscus-Infused Rum
(see page 268)

½ oz. sloe gin

½ oz. pomegranate liqueur

1 oz. fresh grapefruit juice

½ oz. fresh lemon juice

½ oz. Demerara Syrup
(see page 256)

1. Place all of the ingredients in a cocktail shaker, fill it two-thirds of the way with ice, and shake vigorously until chilled.

2. Fill the Collins glass with crushed ice and strain the cocktail over it.

3. Garnish the cocktail with the edible flowers and enjoy.

JUNIOR JOHNSON

THE ANISE, VANILLA, AND ALLSPICE-ENRICHED flavor of Amaro Nonino and the Ancho Reyes pair to hold the rum and bourbon together.

¾ oz. Smith & Cross rum

¾ oz. Bulleit bourbon

½ oz. Amaro Nonino

½ oz. Ancho Reyes

½ oz. Passion Fruit Syrup (see page 263)

½ oz. fresh lemon juice

1. Place all of the ingredients in a cocktail shaker, fill it two-thirds of the way with crushed ice, and shake vigorously until chilled.

2. Pour the contents of the shaker into the tiki mug and top the cocktail with more crushed ice.

3. Garnish the cocktail with the fresh mint and enjoy.

SAILOR'S GUILLOTINE

A WONDERFULLY ORCHESTRATED, albeit unexpected, cocktail.

¼ oz. absinthe

1 oz. rhum agricole

½ oz. falernum

½ oz. Green Chartreuse

1 oz. fresh pineapple juice

¾ oz. fresh lime juice

1. Place all of the ingredients in a cocktail shaker, fill it two-thirds of the way with crushed ice, and shake vigorously until chilled.

2. Pour the contents of the shaker into the tiki mug and top the cocktail with more crushed ice.

3. Garnish the cocktail with the fresh mint and star anise pod and enjoy.

THE EXPEDITION

A CELEBRATION of the ingredients that Donn Beach was exposed to during the travels of his youth, and celebrated for the rest of his ife—coffee and bourbon from New Orleans, fresh citrus from California, and rum and spices from the Caribbean.

2 oz. Hamilton Guyana 86 rum

1 oz. bourbon

¼ oz. Bittermens New Orleans Coffee Liqueur

1 oz. fresh lime juice

½ oz. Cinnamon Syrup (see page 260)

½ oz. Honey Syrup (see page 269)

¼ oz. Vanilla Syrup (see page 259)

2 oz. seltzer

1. Place all of the ingredients in a cocktail shaker, add crushed ice, and flash mix with a hand blender.

2. Pour the contents of the shaker into the tiki mug.

3. Garnish with the edible orchid and enjoy.

SOUTHERN SHIPWRECK

SOME PEOPLE will never purchase a bourbon made outside of Kentucky, which is a shame because the distillery boom has led to quality bourbons being produced all over the country, with Texas' Garrison Brothers standing as one of the very best.

Sugar, for the rim

1 oz. Wray & Nephew rum

1 oz. Garrison Brothers bourbon

¾ oz. fresh lime juice

¾ oz. Orgeat (see page 258)

¼ oz. Brown Sugar Syrup (see page 270)

5 dashes of Scrappy's Chocolate Bitters

1. Rim the coupe with sugar and set it aside.

2. Place all of the ingredients in a cocktail shaker, fill it two-thirds of the way with ice, and shake vigorously until chilled.

3. Strain the cocktail into the rimmed coupe and enjoy.

KAGANO

UMESU IS THE JUICE collected while making umeboshi, or salt-cured ume plums. Here, its salty, sour, and unique flavor binds all of the other elements together.

1½ oz. Santa Teresa 1796 rum

½ oz. umesu

½ oz. blended scotch

¼ oz. banana liqueur

Dash of Saline Solution (see page 270)

1 slice of orange peel

1. Chill the cocktail glass in the freezer.

2. Place all of the ingredients, except for the orange peel, in a mixing glass, fill it two-thirds of the way with ice, and stir until chilled.

3. Strain the cocktail into the chilled cocktail glass. Express the orange peel over the drink and discard it.

4. Garnish the cocktail with the banana leaves and edible flower and enjoy.

POINCIANA

THE PERFECT DRINK to make when you're trying to work with a new rum, since it will reveal its full character. It's also a must when you've got a rum skeptic present, as it will silence them for good.

1½ oz. Brugal 1888 rum

½ oz. Plantation Pineapple rum

¾ oz. fresh lime juice

¼ oz. pineapple juice

½ oz. Simple Syrup (see page 270)

3 dashes of Angostura Bitters

Pinch of cinnamon

1. Chill the coupe in the freezer.

2. Place all of the ingredients in a cocktail shaker, fill it two-thirds of the way with ice, and shake vigorously until chilled.

3. Strain the cocktail into the chilled coupe, garnish with the lime wheel and nutmeg, and enjoy.

RHUM SWIZZLE

IN A COCKTAIL BOOK filled with outstanding summer sippers, this one stands above them all in terms of refreshment.

1 oz. Watermelon Shrub
(see page 271)

1½ oz. rhum agricole

½ oz. fresh lime juice

½ oz. Demerara Syrup
(see page 256)

½ oz. pineapple juice

1. Fill the tiki mug with pebble ice, add all of the ingredients, and use the swizzle method to combine: place a swizzle stick between your hands, lower the swizzle stick into the drink, and quickly rub your palms together to rotate the stick as you move it up and down in the drink. When frost begins to form on the outside of the tiki mug, the drink is ready.

2. Top the cocktail with more ice, garnish with the slice of watermelon, and enjoy.

ANALOGUE

JEFF "BEACHBUM" BERRY, one of the key figures of the recent tiki revival, says that Hamilton 86 is "one of only six rums a tiki enthusiast will ever need."

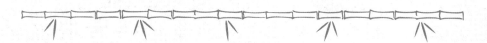

1½ oz. Hamilton Guyana 86 rum

1 oz. bourbon

½ oz. falernum

¼ oz. ginger liqueur

¼ oz. St. Elizabeth Allspice Dram

3 dashes of Angostura Bitters

1. Place all of the ingredients in a mixing glass, fill it two-thirds of the way with ice, and stir until chilled.

2. Fill the rocks glass with crushed ice and strain the cocktail over it.

3. Garnish the cocktail with the apple blossom and enjoy.

THE PINK FLAMINGO

A LOT OF MOVING PARTS here, all of which are synchronized by the Fernet-Branca Reduction.

Splash of Fernet-Branca Reduction (see page 271)

1½ oz. Banks 5 Island Rum

½ oz. Pineapple Syrup (see page 272)

1 oz. freshly brewed hibiscus tea

½ oz. condensed milk

½ oz. cream of coconut

1. Place the reduction in the pilsner glass and set it aside.

2. Place the remaining ingredients and ½ cup ice in a blender and puree until smooth.

3. Pour the contents of the blender into the glass, garnish with the edible flower, and enjoy.

GLASSWARE: Tumbler
GARNISH: Pineapple leaves, dehydrated orange wheel

BEHIND GOD'S BACK

THE SWIZZLE METHOD is not just a bit of show—some bartenders believe it is the best way to mix a drink featuring a handful of ingredients, as it treats them all gently, and still gets them to mingle.

¼ oz. Simple Syrup (see page 270)

¼ oz. Cinnamon Syrup (see page 260)

¼ oz. Orgeat (see page 258)

½ oz. pineapple juice

¾ oz. fresh lime juice

2 oz. Chairman's Reserve rum

2 dashes of Peychaud's Bitters

2 dashes of Angostura Bitters

1. Fill the tumbler with crushed ice, add all of the cocktail ingredients, except for the bitters, and use the swizzle method to combine: place a swizzle stick between your hands, lower the swizzle stick into the drink, and quickly rub your palms together to rotate the stick as you move it up and down in the drink. When frost begins to form on the outside of the vessel, the drink is ready.

2. Add more ice to the glass, top with the bitters, garnish with the pineapple leaves and dehydrated orange wheel, and enjoy.

THE RATTLE & THE RHYTHM

WITH ITS MILD, freshness-packed flavor, jicama juice powers this refreshing serve.

1½ oz. Hamilton Jamaica Gold rum

¾ oz. fresh lime juice

¾ oz. Demerara Syrup (see page 256)

¾ oz. jicama juice

4 fresh mint leaves

Pinch of smoked sea salt

2 dashes of coffee bitters

1. Place all of the ingredients in a cocktail shaker, fill it two-thirds of the way with ice, and shake vigorously until chilled.

2. Fill the rocks glass with crushed ice and strain the cocktail over it.

3. Garnish the cocktail with the fresh mint and enjoy.

GLASSWARE: Brandy snifter

GARNISH: Pineapple chunk, maraschino cherry

THE ESCAPE

A BIT OF INVALUABLE ADVICE: Antica Formula is the best sweet vermouth option, for this and every drink.

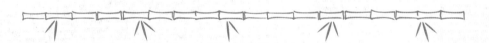

2 oz. El Dorado Single Barrel rum

1 oz. pineapple juice

1 oz. cream of coconut

¾ oz. sweet vermouth

1. Place the rum, pineapple juice, and cream of coconut in a cocktail shaker, fill it two-thirds of the way with ice, and shake vigorously until chilled.

2. Fill the brandy snifter with crushed ice and strain the cocktail over it.

3. Float the vermouth on top of the cocktail, pouring it over the back of a spoon.

4. Garnish with the pineapple chunk and maraschino cherry and enjoy.

HEADLESS HORSEMAN

EVERYONE THINKS summertime and warm weather when it comes to tiki, but this drink is made for the crisp evenings that autumn is known for.

1½ oz. Pumpkin Syrup (see page 272)

¾ oz. cream of coconut

¾ oz. coconut milk

1½ oz. cachaça

¾ oz. fresh orange juice

½ oz. St. Elizabeth Allspice Dram

¾ oz. Cinnamon Syrup (see page 260)

¾ oz. fresh lime juice

1. Place all of the ingredients in a blender, add ½ cup ice, and puree until smooth.

2. Pour the cocktail into the tiki mug and top it with crushed ice.

3. Garnish with the Flaming Lime Shell, wait until the flames go out, and enjoy.

MUTINY OF CLOWNS

CYNAR, AN AMARO made from artichokes and a dozen other plants and herbs, is bitter, as you might expect. But it also has a rich, caramelly note that makes it fast friends with the Black Strap rum.

¾ oz. Cruzan Black Strap rum

¾ oz. Cynar

¾ oz. fresh lime juice

½ oz. Ginger Syrup
(see page 273)

¼ oz. Demerara Syrup
(see page 256)

1. Place all of the ingredients in a cocktail shaker, fill it two-thirds of the way with ice, and shake vigorously until chilled.

2. Double-strain the cocktail into the double rocks glass containing no ice.

3. Set the orange wheel on top of the cocktail, carefully place a dash of 151-proof rum on top of the orange wheel, and use a long match or wand lighter to ignite the rum. Wait until the flames have gone out to enjoy the cocktail.

BARON OF BROOKLYN

FINISHING RUM in Port casks is gaining popularity with distillers. This cocktail asks, "Why wait?" and gives you the happy marriage of these two flavors straightaway.

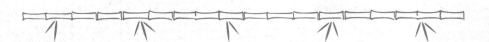

Dash of Bittermens Xocolatl Mole Bitters

Dash of Angostura Bitters

½ oz. Suze

½ oz. banana liqueur

1½ oz. tawny Port

1½ oz. cachaça

1. Place all of the ingredients in a mixing glass, fill it two-thirds of the way with ice, and stir until chilled.

2. Place a large ice cube in the brandy snifter and strain the cocktail over it.

3. Garnish the cocktail with the lemon twist and enjoy.

MARTIKI 2.0

THE ROCK CANDY SYRUP popularized by the Mai Tai at Trader Vic's makes its way into this refreshing swizzle.

1 oz. Wray & Nephew rum

½ oz. Rock Candy Syrup (see page 259)

½ oz. fresh lime juice

1½ oz. pineapple juice

½ oz. El Dorado 3 Year rum

1. Place all of the ingredients, except for the El Dorado rum, in the tiki mug, fill it with crushed ice, and use the swizzle method to combine: place a swizzle stick between your hands, lower the swizzle stick into the drink, and quickly rub your palms together to rotate the stick as you move it up and down in the drink. When frost begins to form on the outside of the vessel, the drink is ready.

2. Top the cocktail with more crushed ice and then float the El Dorado rum on top, pouring it over the back of a spoon.

3. Garnish the cocktail with the pineapple leaves and enjoy.

COTTON MOUTH KILLER

FOR THE RUM BLEND, consider using a few lighter rums such as The Real McCoy 3 Year and Havana Club with some heavier, aged pot still rums like Plantation Xaymaca to create a drink with an incredibly smooth profile.

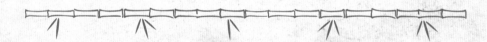

1¾ oz. rum blend

2 teaspoons apricot liqueur

2 teaspoons Galliano

2 teaspoons Demerara Syrup (see page 256)

1 oz. apple juice

1⅜ oz. guava juice

2 bar spoons of Blue Wray & Nephew (see page 271)

1. Place all of the ingredients in a cocktail shaker, except for the Blue Wray & Nephew, fill it two-thirds of the way with ice, and shake vigorously until chilled.

2. Fill the tiki mug with crushed ice and strain the cocktail over it.

3. Top the cocktail with additional crushed ice and gently stir the cocktail.

4. Drizzle the Blue Wray & Nephew over the cocktail and enjoy.

LONDON HAZE

A DRINK THAT will clear away the fog, and leave you feeling uplifted and cosseted.

1 oz. Pineapple-Infused Sailor Jerry (see page 273)

1 oz. Santa Teresa 1796 rum

1 oz. passion fruit puree

¾ oz. fresh lime juice

¾ oz. Vanilla Syrup (see page 259)

1. Place all of the ingredients in a cocktail shaker, fill it two-thirds of the way with ice, and shake vigorously until chilled.

2. Fill the tumbler with crushed ice and double-strain the cocktail over it.

3. Garnish the cocktail with the lit joint, unless, of course, it's illegal, and enjoy.

TRINIDAD SWIZZLE

EASY DRINKING and incredibly refreshing, with the sweetness countered brilliantly by the lime and passion fruit.

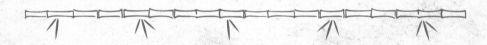

1 oz. Hamilton Jamaica Gold rum

¾ oz. dark rum

2 teaspoons peach liqueur

½ oz. fresh lime juice

2 teaspoons Raspberry & Pomegranate Shrub (see page 273)

½ oz. passion fruit puree

1. Fill the Collins glass with crushed ice. Add all of the ingredients and stir until chilled.

2. Garnish with the orange slice, Luxardo cherry, and fresh mint and enjoy.

CRAB BAY

A SOFT, SWEET DRINK with exhilarating spicy notes and a deep vein of vanilla. If you can't procure this exact brand of CBD syrup, add a drop or two of regular CBD oil to a Banana Syrup (see page 267).

3 dashes of Bittermens 'Elemakule Tiki Bitters

1¼ oz. El Dorado 3 Year rum

¾ oz. Spiced Rum (see page 274)

¼ oz. Behind This Wall Banana CBD Syrup

Pear calvados, to mist

1. Place the bitters, rums, and a large block of ice in the rocks glass.

2. Add the syrup and stir until the cocktail is chilled.

3. Pour a bit of pear calvados into a spray bottle and mist the cocktail with it.

4. Garnish with the dehydrated banana chip and enjoy.

THE SAN FRANCISCO TREAT

BANANA AND FERNET-BRANCA? It isn't a natural pairing, but it manages to work wonders here.

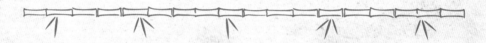

1½ oz. Wray & Nephew rum

¾ oz. banana liqueur

¼ oz. Fernet-Branca

½ oz. fresh lime juice

1 bar spoon of Demerara Syrup (see page 256)

3 dashes of chocolate bitters

1. Chill the Nick & Nora glass in the freezer.

2. Place all of the ingredients in a cocktail shaker, fill it two-thirds of the way with ice, and shake vigorously until chilled.

3. Strain the cocktail into the chilled glass, garnish with the lime wheel and Luxardo cherry, and enjoy.

LOW GRAVITY

JUST ONE HIT of this high-octane treat will mellow out even the most stone-faced individual.

1 oz. Cruzan Estate Diamond rum

½ oz. Whaler's Vanille rum

½ oz. Wray & Nephew rum

½ oz. fresh lime juice

2 oz. guava nectar

½ oz. Appleton Estate Reserve Blend rum

1. Fill the pilsner glass with crushed ice and add all of the ingredients, except for the Appleton Estate rum.

2. Pour the contents of the glass into a cocktail shaker, shake vigorously until chilled, and then pour the cocktail back into the pilsner glass.

3. Float the Appleton Estate rum on top of the cocktail, pouring it over the back of a spoon.

4. Garnish the cocktail with the vanilla bean and edible flower and enjoy.

SCURVY

DOES THIS BRISK BRACER cure it or cause it? Drink a couple and you will have the answer to this question, and many others.

2 oz. Cruzan Citrus rum

1½ oz. Cruzan Light rum

1 oz. Cruzan Coconut rum

Dash of Angostura Bitters

2 oz. pineapple juice

2 oz. Sweet & Sour
(see page 261)

¼ oz. cream of coconut

Dash of Demerara Syrup
(see page 256)

5 lime wedges

6 fresh mint leaves

Pinch of Hawaiian red
alaea salt

2 oz. club soda, to top

1. Place all of the ingredients, except for the club soda, in a cocktail shaker, and gently muddle.

2. Fill the shaker two-thirds of the way with ice and shake vigorously until chilled.

3. Fill the brandy snifter with crushed ice and strain the cocktail over it.

4. Top the cocktail with the club soda, garnish with the strip of grapefruit peel and fresh mint, and enjoy.

BLUE MARINER

A SIMPLE SERVE with a flavor that still manages to go deep.

1½ oz. Wray & Nephew rum

1 oz. Blue Mariner Curaçao
(see page 274)

1 oz. pineapple juice

1 oz. fresh lime juice

1. Place all of the ingredients in a cocktail shaker, add 1 or 2 ice cubes, and whip shake vigorously until chilled.

2. Fill the brandy snifter with crushed ice and strain the cocktail over it.

3. Garnish the cocktail with the Flaming Lime Shell, pineapple leaves, and edible flowers and enjoy.

TUXEDO SITUATION

WITH ITS AMPED-UP sweetness and seductive aroma, satsuma juice is well worth considering when searching for a citrus component that can lend a cocktail something unique.

1½ oz. cachaça

8 fresh cilantro leaves

1 oz. fresh satsuma juice, strained

½ oz. Demerara Syrup (see page 256)

Prosecco, to top

1. Chill the coupe in the freezer.

2. Place all of the ingredients, except for the Prosecco, in a cocktail shaker, fill it two-thirds of the way with ice, and shake vigorously until chilled.

3. Double-strain the cocktail into the chilled coupe and top with Prosecco.

4. Garnish with the satsuma twist and enjoy.

BRILHANTINA

ICED HIBISCUS TEA is as beautiful as it is refreshing. In the summertime, you should always have some in the refrigerator, even more so because it allows you to make this delicious concoction anytime you want.

1½ oz. rhum agricole or cachaça

1¾ oz. iced hibiscus tea

2 teaspoons Demerara Syrup (see page 256)

½ oz. fresh lime juice

½ oz. falernum

Dash of Peychaud's Bitters

1. Place all of the ingredients in a cocktail shaker, fill it two-thirds of the way with ice, and shake vigorously until chilled.

2. Fill the rocks glass with ice and strain the cocktail over it.

3. Garnish the cocktail with the lime wheel and enjoy.

BRILHANTINA
see page 171

THE ISLAND IS CALLING

VERJUS, THE JUICE of unripe wine grapes, is becoming an increasingly common cocktail component, as it is capable of adding sourness without also adding acid to the equation.

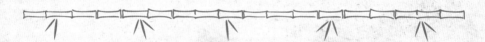

¼ oz. Pineapple Syrup (see page 272)

2 oz. Plantation Pineapple rum

1½ oz. verjus

¼ oz. Smith & Cross rum

1 strip of lime peel

1. Chill the coupe in the freezer.

2. Place all of the ingredients, except for the lime peel, in a mixing glass, fill it two-thirds of the way with ice, and stir until chilled.

3. Strain the cocktail into the chilled coupe, express the strip of lime peel over the cocktail, discard the lime peel, and enjoy the cocktail.

GLASSWARE: Coupe
GARNISH: Strip of orange peel

THINKING OF YOU

FIND YOURSELF a quiet spot and take your time with this one, as it runs in an astonishing number of directions.

1½ oz. cachaça

¾ oz. pineapple juice

½ oz. fresh lemon juice

½ oz. Grenadine
(see page 256)

2 dashes of orange bitters

Dash of Angostura Bitters

1. Chill the coupe in the freezer.

2. Place all of the ingredients in a cocktail shaker, fill it two-thirds of the way with ice, and shake vigorously until chilled.

3. Double-strain the cocktail into the chilled coupe, express the strip of orange peel over the cocktail, use it as a garnish, and enjoy.

HAWAIIAN WAR CHANT

DON THE BEACHCOMBER loved to incorporate anise-flavored spirits into his creations, and loved Herbsaint in particular. Absinthe or Pernod can work here, but the crisp finish of Herbsaint is inimitable.

2 oz. Santa Teresa 1796 rum

¼ oz. grapefruit liqueur

¼ oz. Cinnamon Syrup
(see page 260)

Dash of Angostura Bitters

Dash of Herbsaint

1. Place all of the ingredients in a mixing glass, fill it two-thirds of the way with ice, and stir until chilled.

2. Fill the rocks glass with ice and strain the cocktail over it.

3. Garnish the cocktail with the orange twist and enjoy.

SEA BEAST

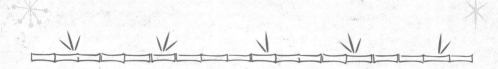

IF YOU CANNOT track down the Rhum Clément Sirop de Canne, you can substitute Demerara Syrup (see page 256).

¾ oz. fresh lime juice

¾ oz. passion fruit puree

¾ oz. Fernet-Branca

1 oz. Rhum Clément Sirop de Canne

1½ oz. Diplomático Reserva rum

1. Place all of the ingredients in a cocktail shaker, fill it two-thirds of the way with ice, and shake vigorously until chilled.

2. Fill the Collins glass with crushed ice, strain the cocktail over it, and enjoy.

MONKEY'S UNCLE

BITTERSWEET WITH notes of coffee, chestnuts, and honey, Amaro Sibilla honors the quality rums utilized here.

1 oz. El Dorado 12 Year rum

1 oz. Santa Teresa 1796 rum

½ oz. Amaro Sibilla

½ oz. banana liqueur

2 dashes of Bittermens 'Elemakule Tiki Bitters

1. Place the ingredients in a mixing glass, fill it two-thirds of the way with ice, and stir until chilled.

2. Fill the tiki mug or double rocks glass with crushed ice and strain the cocktail over it.

3. Garnish the cocktail with the orange wheel, Luxardo cherry, and fresh mint and enjoy.

MONKEY'S UNCLE
see page 179

LEE ROY SELMON

AS LARGE, FEARSOME, and memorable as the NFL legend it is named after.

1 oz. Caña Brava 7 Year rum

1 oz. Galliano

¼ oz. Herbsaint

¼ oz. fresh orange juice

¼ oz. fresh lemon juice

¼ oz. Demerara Syrup (see page 256)

3 dashes of Peychaud's Bitters

1 egg white

1. Chill the cocktail glass in the freezer.

2. Place the ingredients in a cocktail shaker, fill it two-thirds of the way with ice, and shake vigorously until chilled.

3. Strain the cocktail, discard the ice in the shaker, return the cocktail to the shaker, and dry shake for 5 to 7 seconds.

4. Pour the cocktail into the chilled cocktail glass, garnish with the additional Peychaud's Bitters, and enjoy.

MANIGORDO

THE FLORAL NATURE of chamomile, the powerful character of bergamot, and a trio of Plantation rums unite to forge an unforgettable cocktail.

½ oz. Chamomile Syrup
(see page 275)

½ oz. Plantation 3 Stars rum

½ oz. Plantation Pineapple
rum

½ oz. Plantation O.F.T.D. rum

½ oz. fresh lime juice

½ oz. bergamot liqueur

3 dashes of Angostura Bitters

1 oz. pineapple juice

1. Place all of the ingredients in a cocktail shaker, fill it two-thirds of the way with ice, and shake vigorously until chilled.

2. Fill the tiki mug with crushed ice and strain the cocktail over it.

3. Garnish the cocktail with the pineapple leaves, nutmeg, and orange wedge and enjoy.

KAMA'AINA

THE #9 MIX is poised become your favorite secret weapon, adding richness, spice, and an eye-catching froth to drinks.

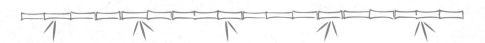

½ oz. #9 (see page 275)

1 oz. Spiced Rum
(see page 274)

1 oz. rhum agricole

1 oz. guava nectar

½ oz. cream of coconut

½ oz. fresh lime juice

2 dashes of Angostura Bitters

1. Place all of the ingredients, except for the bitters, in a cocktail shaker, fill it two-thirds of the way with crushed ice, and shake vigorously until chilled.

2. Pour the contents of the shaker into the Collins glass and top the cocktail with the bitters.

3. Garnish the cocktail with the orchid and enjoy.

DOT LINE

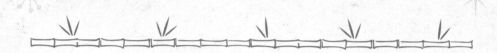

A RICH, FRUITY, spicy cocktail that's good any time of day.

¼ oz. ground Kenyan coffee

1⅓ oz. Bacardí Carta Blanca rum

⅔ oz. umeshu

1 bar spoon of Pedro Ximénez sherry

1 bar spoon of St-Germain

Dash of balsamic vinegar

1. Place a coffee dripper over a mixing glass, line the coffee dripper with a filter, and place the coffee in the filter.

2. Pour the rum, umeshu, sherry, and St-Germain over the coffee and let them drip into the glass.

3. Add the balsamic vinegar to the mixing glass, then ice, and stir to incorporate.

4. Place an ice sphere in the rocks glass, strain the cocktail over it, and enjoy.

ZU ZU

TIKI HAS ALWAYS BEEN a large part of cocktail culture in Miami, as this drink, which goes back to Club Luau, a popular spot in the '50s, shows.

2 oz. Diplomático
Reserva rum

½ oz. Plantation
Pineapple rum

½ oz. fresh lime juice

½ oz. fresh grapefruit juice

½ oz. fresh orange juice

1 oz. #9 (see page 275)

4 pineapple chunks

1. Place the ingredients in a blender, add ½ cup ice, and puree until smooth.

2. Pour the cocktail into the brandy snifter, garnish with the cinnamon and orange peel, and enjoy.

DREAMFLOWER

LEADING WITH VANILLA and backed up by notes of citrus and cinnamon, Licor 43 was made to become part of your tiki arsenal.

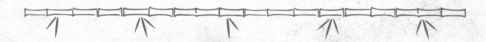

1 oz. Appleton Estate Reserve Blend rum

1 oz. Santa Teresa 1796 rum

2 oz. fresh pineapple juice

½ oz. Licor 43

½ oz. agave nectar

2 drops of Angostura Bitters

1. Chill the coupe in the freezer.

2. Place the ingredients in a cocktail shaker, fill it two-thirds of the way with ice, and shake vigorously until chilled.

3. Double-strain the cocktail into the chilled coupe, garnish with the freshly grated nutmeg, and enjoy.

OCCHI SU DI ME

COECOEI, A LIQUEUR from Aruba, has a distinctive red color derived from the sap of the kukwisa, an agave plant found on the island. Here it pairs with overproof rum and banana liqueur to make for a memorable summer cocktail.

½ oz. Hamilton Guyana 151 rum

¼ oz. vodka

⅛ oz. coecoei

⅛ oz. banana liqueur

½ oz. fresh orange juice

½ oz. cranberry juice

½ oz. pineapple juice

Splash of Grenadine (see page 256)

Splash of Grand Marnier

1. Place all of the ingredients in a cocktail shaker, fill it two-thirds of the way with ice, and shake vigorously until chilled.

2. Fill the Collins glass with ice and strain the cocktail into it.

3. Garnish the cocktail with the hibiscus blossom and lime wedge and enjoy.

DESERT LILY

BITTER, FRESH, and citrusy, aloe vera juice makes this cocktail bright and refreshing.

2 oz. Mount Gay Black Barrel rum

1 oz. aloe vera juice

¾ oz. fresh lime juice

¾ oz. Demerara Syrup (see page 256)

½ oz. kiwi puree

¼ oz. fresh lemon juice

3 drops of Fee Brothers Lavender Flower Water

1. Place all of the ingredients in a blender, add ½ cup ice, and puree until smooth.

2. Pour the cocktail into the tiki mug, top with crushed ice, garnish with the Luxardo cherry, and enjoy.

GLASSWARE: Nick & Nora glass

GARNISH: Sage leaves

BURNT SAGE SOUR

PLANTATION O.F.T.D. is a blend of rums from Guyana, Jamaica, and Barbados. The letters stand for Old Fashioned Traditional Dark, and, considering its funky, rich flavor and aroma, that moniker is right on the mark.

1 oz. Burnt Sugar Syrup (see page 276)

1 oz. Ancho Reyes

1 oz. Plantation O.F.T.D. rum

1 oz. pineapple juice

½ oz. fresh lime juice

1. Chill the Nick & Nora glass in the freezer.

2. Place all of the ingredients in a cocktail shaker, fill it two-thirds of the way with ice, and shake vigorously until chilled.

3. Double-strain the cocktail into the chilled Nick & Nora glass.

4. Torch the sage leaves, garnish the cocktail with them, and enjoy.

BALINESE ROOM #2

DIMMI MEANS "tell me" in Italian. That's fitting in this cocktail, which has quite a story to regale those who imbibe.

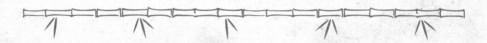

Absinthe, to rinse

1 oz. Plantation 5 Year rum

1 oz. Dimmi Liquore di Milano

1 oz. Yellow Chartreuse

1 oz. fresh lime juice

Dash of Angostura Bitters

1. Chill the Hurricane glass in the freezer.

2. Rinse the chilled glass with the absinthe, swirling to coat, and discard the excess.

3. Place the remaining ingredients in a cocktail shaker, fill it two-thirds of the way with ice, and shake vigorously until chilled.

4. Double-strain the cocktail into the Hurricane glass, garnish with the lime wheel and star anise, and enjoy.

ABSENT STARS

A BITTER, SALTY, FRUITY concoction that communicates tiki's talent for being complex and accessible at the same time.

1 oz. Campari

1 oz. rhum agricole

¾ oz. fresh lemon juice

½ oz. Passion Fruit Syrup (see page 263)

½ oz. apricot liqueur

5 drops of Saline Solution (see page 270)

10 drops of Bittermens Hopped Grapefruit Bitters

1. Place the ingredients in a cocktail shaker, fill it two-thirds of the way with ice, and shake vigorously until chilled.

2. Fill the double rocks glass with crushed ice and strain the cocktail over it.

3. Garnish the cocktail with the orange twist and enjoy.

LITTLE
BLACK STAR

A GOOD ONE to kick off a summertime Sunday brunch with.

1½ oz. Brugal 1888 rum

½ oz. Coffee Syrup
(see page 276)

½ oz. fresh lime juice

¼ oz. curaçao

1 bar spoon of Luxardo
maraschino liqueur

1. Chill the coupe in the freezer.

2. Place the ingredients in a cocktail shaker, fill it two-thirds of the way with ice, and shake vigorously until chilled.

3. Strain the cocktail into the chilled coupe, garnish with the star anise, and enjoy.

DAUPHIN

CONSIDER SAVING THIS for after dinner while sitting by the firepit on a late summer evening.

1½ oz. Goslings Black Seal rum

2 dashes of Miracle Mile Bitters Co. Chocolate Chili Bitters

½ oz. Demerara Syrup (see page 256)

½ oz. Ancho Reyes

1 oz. absinthe

1¼ oz. toasted coconut almond milk

1. Place the Collins glass in a bowl and build the cocktail in the glass, adding the ingredients in the order they are listed.

2. Fill the bowl and the glass with pebble ice and stir the cocktail until it is chilled and combined.

3. Garnish the cocktail with the cacao nibs and star anise and enjoy.

THE NEXT LEVEL

At its heart, tiki is a rum-based art. But the complex and deeply flavored cocktails that have developed around that center have set some of the world's best bartenders on a mission to craft cocktails that utilize tiki's wide array of flavors in drinks built around other spirits.

CITY OF GOLD

INSTEAD OF LOSING your mind in the pursuit of riches, kick back with this cocktail and spend your time in pleasant daydreams.

⅓ bar spoon of aji pepper powder

⅔ teaspoon caster sugar

1 lemon wedge

¼ oz. Solbeso

1 oz. pisco

½ oz. apricot liqueur

¼ oz. fresh lemon juice

1½ oz. Prosecco

1. Chill the coupe in the freezer.

2. Combine the ají pepper powder and caster sugar on a plate. Run the lemon wedge halfway around the rim of the chilled coupe and then rim the glass in the sugar mixture.

3. Place all of the remaining ingredients, except for the Prosecco, in a mixing glass, fill it two-thirds of the way with ice, and stir until chilled.

4. Strain the cocktail into the rimmed glass and top with the Prosecco.

5. Garnish with the orange twist and enjoy.

CHARTREUSE SWIZZLE

A PERFECTLY BALANCED cocktail that will provide the ideal punctuation to a warm spring day spent getting the garden ready.

1½ oz. Green Chartreuse

1 oz. pineapple juice

¾ oz. fresh lime juice

½ oz. falernum

1. Fill the Collins glass with pebble ice. Add all of the ingredients and use the swizzle method to combine: place a swizzle stick between your hands, lower the swizzle stick into the drink, and quickly rub your palms together to rotate the stick as you move it up and down in the drink. When frost begins to form on the outside of the vessel, the drink is ready.

2. Top the cocktail with more pebble ice and enjoy.

FIRE STAR PUNCH

AN OUT-OF-THIS WORLD cocktail, inspired by the diet one will have to follow when humanity colonizes Mars, relying heavily on corn and red peppers.

1 oz. mellow corn whiskey

1 oz. Wild Turkey Rye whiskey

¾ oz. Martini & Rossi Riserva Speciale Rubino

½ oz. Martini & Rossi Bitter

1¼ oz. iced hibiscus tea

½ oz. Red Pepper Syrup (see page 277)

½ oz. Citric Acid Solution (see page 272)

1. Place all of the ingredients in a mixing glass and fill it two-thirds of the way with ice. Using another mixing glass, pour the cocktail back and forth between the glasses three times; the more distance between your glasses, the better. This method of mixing is known as the "Cuban roll."

2. Place a large ice cube in the goblet and strain the cocktail over it.

3. Garnish with the baby corn and cornflower and enjoy.

ABSINTHE-MINDED COCKTAIL

A COCKTAIL that showcases the importance of garnish, charming the drinker with its appealing aesthetics, and then mirroring the flavors present in the drink.

Absinthe, to rinse

2 oz. Plymouth Gin

¾ oz. fresh lime juice

¾ oz. falernum

1. Rinse the coupe with absinthe, swirling to coat, and discard any excess.

2. Place the remaining ingredients in a cocktail shaker, fill it two-thirds of the way with ice, and shake vigorously until chilled.

3. Double-strain the cocktail into the coupe, garnish the drink with the fresh mint and orange twist, and enjoy.

LAWYERS, GUNS & MONEY

A COCKTAIL FILLED with romance, danger, and intrigue.

1½ oz. Côtes du Rhône

½ oz. ruby Port

½ oz. Pedro Ximénez sherry

½ oz. Rhum Barbancourt 5 Star

2 dashes of Amargo Chuncho bitters

2 dashes of Bittermens Hellfire Habanero Shrub

¼ oz. crème de cacao

1. Place all of the ingredients in a cocktail shaker, fill it two-thirds of the way with ice, and shake vigorously until chilled.

2. Fill the rocks glass with pebble ice and strain the cocktail over it.

3. Garnish the cocktail with the cocoa powder, chili powder, and orange twist and enjoy.

CAPTAIN AWESOME

WITH ALMONDS, apricot, and coconut winding through it, Mahiki makes for a tiki sensation.

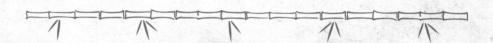

2 cucumber slices

1 oz. London Dry gin

1 oz. fresh lemon juice

½ oz. Ancho Reyes

½ oz. Mahiki Coconut Rum Liqueur

½ oz. Demerara Syrup (see page 256)

1 oz. pineapple juice

1. Place the cucumber slices in a cocktail shaker and muddle.

2. Add the remaining ingredients, fill the shaker two-thirds of the way with ice, and shake vigorously until chilled.

3. Place a large ice cube in the rocks glass and strain the cocktail over it.

4. Garnish the cocktail with the slice of cucumber and enjoy.

EMULS

SOME SHŌCHŪ PRODUCERS bottle the "heads" of their distillation, the first part that distillers usually discard. Called hanatare, it is potent and intense. Washing it with brown butter helps it, and you, take the edge off.

Finely grated coconut, for the rim

1⅓ oz. Brown Butter–Washed Hanatare Shōchū
(see page 277)

½ oz. fresh lemon juice

⅛ oz. pineapple juice

1 bar spoon of Orgeat
(see page 258)

½ bar spoon of white sesame oil

1. Rim the champagne flute with coconut.

2. Place all of the remaining ingredients in a cocktail shaker and emulsify them with a hand blender.

3. Double-strain the cocktail into the champagne flute and enjoy.

CHERRY CHERRY MONKEY

THE SALTED PISTACHIO SYRUP is good enough that it can be used in just about everything. That's a lucky break, as you'll want to try using it in everything after your initial encounter.

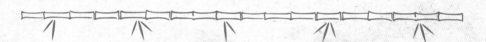

1½ oz. Monkey Shoulder Blended Scotch Whisky

1 oz. Salted Pistachio Syrup (see page 278)

½ oz. fresh lime juice

8 to 10 cherries

5 drops of shiso bitters or 1 bar spoon of Dover Shiso Liqueur

1. Place all of the ingredients in a mason jar and use a hand blender to emulsify the mixture.

2. Strain the mixture into a cocktail shaker, fill it two-thirds of the way with ice, and shake vigorously until chilled.

3. Place a large ice cube in the brandy snifter and strain the cocktail over it.

4. Garnish the cocktail with the shiso leaf and edible flowers and enjoy.

PANDA LATINO

HERBAL, SOUR, and ever-so-slightly salty, this cocktail is the perfect lead-in to a multicourse dinner party out on the patio.

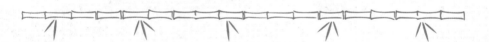

²⁄₃ oz. gin

1 kiwi fruit, peeled

1⅓ oz. Herb Tea
(see page 278)

²⁄₃ oz. St-Germain

2 bar spoons of fresh lemon juice

⅓ teaspoon freshly grated Parmesan cheese

1. Place all of the ingredients in a mason jar and use a hand blender to emulsify the mixture.

2. Fill the double rocks glass with crushed ice and pour the cocktail over it.

3. Top the drink with more crushed ice, garnish with the kiwi and rosemary, and enjoy.

LIQUID SUNSHINE

IF YOU LIKE pisco punch, you'll love this brilliant tiki-tinged riff.

1½ oz. Coconut Butter–
Washed Pisco (see page 280)

¾ oz. Passion Fruit Syrup
(see page 263)

¾ oz. fresh lime juice

Hibiscus Tincture
(see page 278), to taste

1. Chill the coupe in the freezer.

2. Place all of the ingredients, except for the tincture, in a cocktail shaker, fill it two-thirds of the
way with ice, and shake vigorously until chilled.

3. Double-strain the cocktail into the chilled
coupe, add a few drops of Hibiscus Tincture,
and enjoy.

TENTATION

RESIDING SOMEWHERE between shōchū and gin, tumugi is capable of working wonders when paired with tropical fruits.

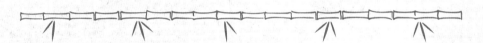

¾ oz. Wapirits Tumugi

½ oz. lychee liqueur

2 bar spoons of peach liqueur

2 bar spoons of mango puree

1 bar spoon of Monin Elderflower Syrup

2 bar spoons of fresh lemon juice

⅓ bar spoon of ginger juice

Pinch of ground cardamom

2 dashes of Bob's Abbotts Bitters

1. Chill the cocktail glass in the freezer.

2. Place all of the ingredients in a cocktail shaker, fill it two-thirds of the way with ice, and shake vigorously until chilled.

3. Double-strain the cocktail into the chilled cocktail glass, garnish it with the peppercorns, and enjoy.

PIÑA FUMADA

ANY MEZCAL will work in this drink, but Quiquiriqui, with its peppery finish, is the best option to counter all the spice and sweetness.

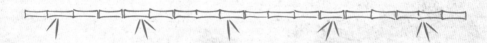

1¼ oz. mezcal

¾ oz. fresh lemon juice

2 teaspoons falernum

½ oz. honey

Club soda, to top

1. Place all of the ingredients, except for the club soda, in a cocktail shaker, fill it two-thirds of the way with ice, and shake vigorously until chilled.

2. Fill the Collins glass with crushed ice and strain the cocktail over it.

3. Top the cocktail with club soda and more crushed ice. Garnish with the pineapple leaf and lemon wedge and enjoy.

GLASS OFF

INSPIRED BY THE EPIC TUNE from Bernie Leadon—best known as one of the founding members of the Eagles—this cocktail will whisk you away to some charming remove.

1 oz. mezcal

¾ oz. Aperol

⅞ oz. fresh lime juice

½ oz. Demerara Syrup (see page 256)

1¼ oz. pineapple juice

3 dashes of absinthe

1 egg white

1. Place all of the ingredients in a cocktail shaker containing no ice and dry shake for 15 seconds.

2. Fill the shaker two-thirds of the way with ice and shake vigorously until chilled.

3. Double-strain the cocktail into the large coupe and garnish with the dehydrated pineapple slice.

A BALCONY IN CHIBA

SUBTLE AND SATISFYING, this long, refreshing drink also packs quite a punch.

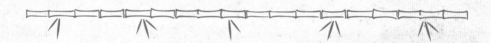

1⅜ oz. shōchū

¾ oz. Suntory Toki Whisky

1 oz. Passion Fruit Cordial
(see page 275)

1 egg white

½ oz. fresh lime juice

½ oz. fresh lemon juice

1. Place all of the ingredients in a cocktail shaker containing no ice and dry shake for 15 seconds.

2. Fill the cocktail shaker two-thirds of the way with ice and shake vigorously until chilled.

3. Fill the Collins glass with ice and strain the cocktail over it.

4. Garnish with the paprika and enjoy.

HERO WATER

A GLOBETROTTING COCKTAIL that will keep you going on your own quest.

2 oz. shōchū

1 oz. fresh cucumber juice

¾ oz. fresh lime juice

¾ oz. cream of coconut

2 dashes of Angostura Bitters

1. Place all of the ingredients in a cocktail shaker, fill it two-thirds of the way with ice, and shake vigorously until chilled.

2. Fill the double rocks glass with ice and strain the cocktail over it.

3. Garnish the cocktail with the lime wheel, cucumber ribbon, and tiki umbrella and enjoy.

VIVA SANTANA

THERE IS NO SHORTAGE of options when falernum is called for, but John D. Taylor's Velvet Falernum, which is produced in Barbados, is the overwhelming choice of tiki's best practitioners.

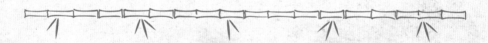

1¾ oz. mezcal

¾ oz. fresh lime juice

½ oz. Orgeat (see page 258)

½ oz. falernum

¼ oz. Passion Fruit Syrup (see page 263)

1. Fill the Collins glass with crushed ice and add all of the ingredients. Use the swizzle method to combine: place a swizzle stick between your hands, lower the swizzle stick into the drink, and quickly rub your palms together to rotate the stick as you move it up and down in the drink. When frost begins to form on the outside of the vessel, the drink is ready.

2. Top the cocktail with more crushed ice, garnish with the lime wheel and dehydrated passion fruit slice, and enjoy.

ALABASTER CAVERNS

WHEN THE SUMMER heat stops being pleasant and starts to overwhelm, reach for this wintry serve.

1½ oz. Cutty Sark

½ oz. sherry

½ oz. Cinnamon Syrup
(see page 260)

Dash of Angostura Bitters

½ oz. fresh lime juice

½ oz. pineapple juice

½ oz. coconut milk

½ oz. cream of coconut

1. Place all of the ingredients in a cocktail shaker, add 3 ice cubes, and whip shake vigorously until chilled.

2. Fill the pilsner glass with crushed ice and strain the cocktail over it.

3. Garnish the cocktail with the pineapple leaves and pineapple wedge and enjoy.

FIRE WALK WITH ME

A SIMPLE COCKTAIL capable of taking on numerous guises.

½ oz. fresh lime juice

½ oz. Orgeat (see page 258)

2 jalapeño pepper slices

2 oz. reposado tequila

½ oz. falernum

1. Place the lime juice, Orgeat, and jalapeño in a cocktail shaker and muddle.

2. Add the tequila and falernum, fill the cocktail shaker two-thirds of the way with ice, and shake vigorously until chilled.

3. Fill the rocks glass with crushed ice, strain the cocktail over it, and enjoy.

GLASSWARE: Coupe

GARNISH: Freshly grated nutmeg

MR. OCTOBER

SKIP THE PUMPKIN COCKTAILS that become ubiquitous once fall arrives, and reach for this beautifully balanced serve.

1½ oz. applejack

¾ oz. Cinnamon Syrup (see page 260)

¾ oz. fresh lemon juice

½ oz. Galliano

2 dashes of St. Elizabeth Allspice Dram

1. Chill the coupe in the freezer.

2. Place all of the ingredients in a cocktail shaker, fill it two-thirds of the way with ice, and shake vigorously until chilled.

3. Double-strain the cocktail into the chilled coupe, garnish with the freshly grated nutmeg, and enjoy.

ASYLUM HARBOR

AN INVENTIVE CONCOCTION from one of tiki's modern masters, Martin Cate.

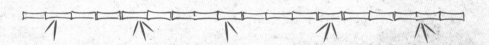

1¼ oz. Damrak gin

½ oz. Benedictine

¼ oz. almond liqueur

1 bar spoon of St. Elizabeth Allspice Dram

½ oz. Ginger Syrup (see page 273)

½ oz. passion fruit puree

½ oz. fresh lime juice

¾ oz. grapefruit juice

1. Place all of the ingredients in a cocktail shaker, fill it two-thirds of the way with ice, and shake vigorously until chilled.

2. Fill the Collins glass with ice and strain the cocktail over it.

3. Garnish the cocktail with the bitters, nutmeg, fresh mint, and grapefruit twist and enjoy.

BEAU SOIR

BY TAKING THE simple step of adding two kinds of bitters, the Chartreuse Swizzle, which is famous for its balance, comes into possession of exceptional depth.

2 oz. Green Chartreuse

1¼ oz. pineapple juice

¾ oz. fresh lime juice

½ oz. falernum

2 dashes of Angostura Bitters

2 dashes of Peychaud's Bitters

1. Fill the Collins glass with crushed ice, add all of the ingredients, except for the bitters, and use the swizzle method to combine: place a swizzle stick between your hands, lower the swizzle stick into the drink, and quickly rub your palms together to rotate the stick as you move it up and down in the drink. When frost begins to form on the outside of the vessel, the drink is ready.

2. Top the cocktail with the bitters, garnish it with the fresh mint, and enjoy.

ONE OF THESE NIGHTS

CAPABLE OF CARRYING Sunday brunch where you always secretly hope it will go: pleasantly into the evening.

1¼ oz. Amaro Lucano

¾ oz. Cognac

¼ oz. curaçao

¼ oz. fresh lemon juice

½ oz. Orgeat (see page 258)

¾ oz. cold-brew coffee

Dash of Peychaud's Bitters

1. Chill the coupe in the freezer.

2. Place all of the ingredients in a cocktail shaker, fill it two-thirds of the way with ice, and shake vigorously until chilled.

3. Double-strain the cocktail into the chilled coupe.

4. Gently torch the star anise, garnish the cocktail with it, and enjoy.

THE NUTTY, DEEPLY SAVORY Manzanilla sherry and Japanese whisky are gently tied together by the Papaya Shrub.

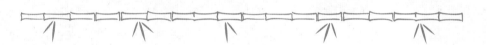

1½ oz. Manzanilla sherry

½ oz. White Oak Akashi Japanese Whisky

½ oz. Papaya Shrub (see page 279)

½ oz. Cardamaro

2 dashes of Dale DeGroff's Aromatic Pimento Bitters

1. Place all of the ingredients in a cocktail shaker, fill it two-thirds of the way with ice, and shake vigorously until chilled.

2. Fill the Collins glass with crushed ice, strain the cocktail over it, and enjoy.

THE ROBIN'S NEST

A TOUCH OF CRANBERRY JUICE makes this drink perfect for the fall, when you first feel the summer slipping away, and winter approaching.

1 oz. Suntory Toki Japanese Whisky

½ oz. Plantation O.F.T.D. rum

½ oz. Cinnamon Syrup (see page 260)

½ oz. fresh lemon juice

¾ oz. pineapple juice

1 oz. Passion Fruit Honey (see page 279)

1 oz. cranberry juice

1. Place all of the ingredients, except for the cranberry juice, in a cocktail shaker, fill it two-thirds of the way with ice, and shake vigorously until chilled.

2. Fill the hurricane glass with crushed ice and top with the cranberry juice.

3. Garnish the cocktail with the candied pineapple wedge, cherry, and tiki umbrella.

HISTORIA DE UN AMOR

ONE FOR THOSE who find themselves torn between their loves for agave spirits and tiki.

1½ oz. tequila

½ oz. mezcal

¾ oz. fresh lime juice

¾ oz. Pineapple Syrup
(see page 272)

¼ oz. Passion Fruit Syrup
(see page 263)

5 dashes of Thai Chili Tincture
(see page 279)

1. Place all of the ingredients in a cocktail shaker, add 2 or 3 ice cubes, and whip shake vigorously until chilled.

2. Fill the tiki mug with crushed ice and strain the cocktail over it.

3. Garnish the cocktail with the Luxardo cherry, pineapple wedge, edible orchid, and pineapple leaves and enjoy.

ISLE OF VIEW

TAKE THE EXAMPLE provided by this drink to heart—a bit of Maldon can go a long way in terms of adding depth to a cocktail.

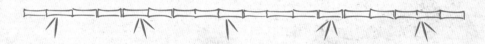

2 oz. Absolut Elyx vodka

¾ oz. Orgeat (see page 258)

¾ oz. fresh lime juice

¾ oz. Passion Fruit Syrup (see page 263)

Pinch of Maldon sea salt

1. Place all of the ingredients in a cocktail shaker, fill it two-thirds of the way with ice, and shake vigorously until chilled.

2. Fill the copper mug with crushed ice and strain the cocktail over it.

3. Garnish the cocktail with the freshly grated nutmeg and fresh mint and enjoy.

FARM & VINE

A UNIQUE COCKTAIL full of ingredients that you typically find gathering dust and rarely have a use for.

1 oz. aquavit

¾ oz. Manzanilla sherry

½ oz. verjus

¾ oz. fresh lime juice

¾ oz. Sugar Snap Pea Syrup (see page 281)

½ oz. egg white

1 oz. Q Elderflower Tonic

1. Place all of the ingredients, except for the elderflower tonic, in a cocktail shaker with no ice and dry shake for 10 seconds.

2. Fill the cocktail shaker two-thirds of the way with ice and shake vigorously until chilled.

3. Add the elderflower tonic to the cocktail shaker, strain the cocktail into the rocks glass, and add a few ice cubes.

4. Garnish the cocktail with the shiso leaf and Umeboshi Powder and enjoy.

UMEBOSHI POWDER: Using a dehydrator on a setting for vegetables, spread pitted and pickled umeboshi plums on a tray and dehydrate for 3 days. This will produce a perfectly dry plum, which can then be ground into a powder.

CHASIN' THE SUNSHINE

HORCHATA LAYS a great foundation for tiki drinks. Spiking it with the vanilla-forward flavor of pear and floral cardamom underscores that attribute even more.

1½ oz. tequila

1 oz. Ancho Reyes

2½ oz. Pear & Cardamom Horchata (see page 280)

½ oz. fresh lime juice

Dash of Angostura Bitters

1. Place all of the ingredients in a cocktail shaker, fill it two-thirds of the way with ice, and shake vigorously until chilled.

2. Fill the clay pot with crushed ice and double-strain the cocktail over it.

3. Garnish the cocktail with the lime wheel, cinnamon stick, and fresh mint and enjoy.

APPENDIX

GRENADINE

2 cups 100 percent pomegranate juice

2 cups sugar

1. Place the pomegranate juice in a saucepan and bring it to a simmer over medium-low heat. Cook until it has reduced by half.

2. Add the sugar and stir until it has dissolved.

3. Remove the pan from heat and let the grenadine cool completely before using or storing in the refrigerator, where it will keep for up to 1 month.

DEMERARA SYRUP

1 cup water

½ cup demerara sugar

1½ cups sugar

1. Place the water in a saucepan and bring it to a boil.

2. Add the sugars and stir until they have dissolved. Remove the pan from heat and let the syrup cool completely before using or storing.

DONN'S MIX

1 cup Honey & Cinnamon Syrup (see page 260)

1 cup grapefruit juice

1. Place the ingredients in a large mason jar and stir to combine.

2. Use immediately or store the mixture in the refrigerator, where it will keep for up to 2 weeks.

LIME CORDIAL

18 ripe limes

3 cups caster (superfine) sugar

1. Rinse the limes with warm water and scrub with your hands or a vegetable brush. Set them on a dish towel to dry.

2. Peel the limes with a vegetable peeler, removing as little of the underlying white pith as possible. Place the peeled limes in the refrigerator to chill overnight.

3. Place the peels in a nonreactive container and add the sugar, making sure that it covers the peels entirely. Cover the container and let it rest overnight.

4. The next day, cut the limes in half and juice them. Add the juice to the lime peel-and-sugar mixture and stir for several minutes, until the sugar has dissolved.

5. Cover the container and refrigerate for at least 12 hours and up to 2 days.

6. Strain the cordial through a fine sieve and chill in the refrigerator for 24 hours before using.

ORGEAT

2 cups almonds

1 cup Demerara Syrup
(see page 256)

1 teaspoon orange blossom
water

2 oz. vodka

1. Preheat the oven to 400°F. Place the almonds on a baking sheet, place them in the oven, and toast until they are fragrant, about 5 minutes. Remove the almonds from the oven and let them cool completely.

2. Place the nuts in a food processor and pulse until they are a coarse meal. Set the almonds aside.

3. Place the syrup in a saucepan and warm it over medium heat. Add the almond meal, remove the pan from heat, and let the mixture steep for 6 hours.

4. Strain the mixture through cheesecloth and discard the solids. Stir in the orange blossom water and vodka. Use the orgeat immediately or store in an airtight container.

PASSION FRUIT BLEND

15 oz. passion fruit puree

1 lb. caster (superfine) sugar

6⅓ oz. Campari

1. Place all of the ingredients in a large mason jar and stir until the sugar has dissolved.

2. Use immediately or store in the refrigerator, where the mixture will keep for up to a month.

ROCK CANDY SYRUP

░░░░░░░░░░░░░░░░░░░░░░░░░░░░░░

½ cup water

1 cup turbinado sugar

1 cinnamon stick

2 whole cloves

1. Place the water in a small saucepan and bring it to a boil.

2. Add the sugar and stir until it has dissolved.

3. Add the cinnamon stick and cloves and return the syrup to a boil. Reduce the heat and simmer the syrup for 15 minutes.

4. Remove the pan from heat and let the syrup cool completely. Strain before using or storing in the refrigerator, where the syrup will keep for up to 6 months.

VANILLA SYRUP

░░░░░░░░░░░░░░░░░░░░░░░░░░░░░░

1 cup water

2 cups sugar

1 vanilla bean

1. Place the water in a small saucepan and bring it to a boil.

2. Add the sugar and stir until it has dissolved. Remove the pan from heat.

3. Halve the vanilla bean and scrape the seeds into the syrup. Cut the vanilla bean pod into thirds and add them to the syrup. Stir to combine, cover the pan, and let it sit at room temperature for 12 hours.

4. Strain the syrup through cheesecloth before using or storing in the refrigerator, where it will keep for up to 6 months.

HONEY & CINNAMON SYRUP

1 cup water

2 cinnamon sticks, halved

1 cup honey

1. Place the water and cinnamon sticks in a saucepan and bring the mixture to a boil.

2. Add the honey and stir until it has liquefied. Remove the pan from heat.

3. Cover the pan and let the syrup sit at room temperature for 12 hours.

4. Strain the syrup through cheesecloth before using or storing in the refrigerator, where it will keep for up to 1 month.

CINNAMON SYRUP

1 cup water

2 cinnamon sticks, halved

2 cups sugar

1. Place the water and cinnamon sticks in a saucepan and bring the mixture to a boil.

2. Add the sugar and stir until it has dissolved. Remove the pan from heat.

3. Cover the pan and let the syrup sit at room temperature for 12 hours.

4. Strain the syrup through cheesecloth before using or storing in the refrigerator, where it will keep for up to 1 month.

CINNAMON & VANILLA SYRUP

1 cup water

2 cinnamon sticks

2⅔ cups sugar

1 vanilla bean

1. Place the water and cinnamon sticks in a saucepan and bring the mixture to a boil.

2. Add the sugar and stir until it has dissolved. Remove the pan from heat.

3. Halve the vanilla bean and scrape the seeds into the syrup. Add the vanilla bean pod and stir to combine. Cover the pan and let the syrup sit at room temperature for 12 hours.

4. Strain the syrup through cheesecloth before using or storing in the refrigerator, where it will keep for up to 6 months.

SWEET & SOUR

2 oz. fresh lemon juice

4 oz. fresh lime juice

6 oz. Demerara Syrup (see page 256)

1. Place all of the ingredients in a mason jar, seal it, and shake until combined.

2. Use immediately or store in the refrigerator, where it will keep for up to 3 months.

RHUBARB SYRUP

1 cup rhubarb puree

2 cups sugar

2 cups water

Zest of ½ lemon

1. Place all of the ingredients in a saucepan and bring the mixture to a boil, stirring to dissolve the sugar.

2. Remove the pan from heat and let the syrup cool completely.

3. Strain the syrup before using or storing in the refrigerator, where it will keep for up to 1 month.

HONEY & GINGER SYRUP

2 cups honey

2 cups water

2⅔ oz. ginger

3 oz. fresh orange juice

1. Place all of the ingredients in a blender and puree until smooth.

2. Strain the syrup before using or storing in the refrigerator, where it will keep for up to 1 month.

CHOCOLATE-INFUSED DON Q 151

2 cups dark chocolate chips

1 (750 ml) bottle of Don Q 151-Proof rum

1. Place the chocolate chips and rum in a large mason jar and let the mixture steep at room temperature for 24 hours.

2. Strain before using or storing.

COCONUT SYRUP

1 cup coconut water

1 cup demerara sugar

1. Place the coconut water in a saucepan and bring it to a boil.

2. Add the sugar and stir until it has dissolved. Remove the pan from heat and let the syrup cool.

3. Use immediately or store in the refrigerator, where it will keep for up to 1 month.

MARLO'S MIX

1 cup St. Elizabeth Allspice Dram

1 cup Cinnamon Syrup (see page 260)

1. Place the ingredients in a mason jar, cover it, and shake until combined.

2. Store in the refrigerator, where it will keep indefinitely.

PASSION FRUIT SYRUP

1½ cups passion fruit puree

1½ cups Demerara Syrup (see page 256)

1. Place the ingredients in a mason jar, cover it, and shake until combined.

2. Store in the refrigerator, where the syrup will keep for up to 1 month.

BANANA & CASHEW ORGEAT

1 cup cashew milk

2 cups sugar

4 oz. banana liqueur

1. Place the cashew milk in a saucepan and bring it to a simmer.

2. Place the sugar in a large mason jar, pour the warm cashew milk over the sugar, and stir until it has dissolved. Let the mixture cool.

3. Stir in the banana liqueur and use immediately or store in the refrigerator, where it will keep for up to 6 months.

PINK ZOMBIE MIX

1 cup Cinnamon & Vanilla Syrup (see page 261)

1 cup falernum

1 cup grapefruit juice

1. Place the ingredients in a mason jar, cover it, and shake until combined.

2. Store in the refrigerator, where it will keep for up to 1 month.

HIBISCUS SYRUP

¼ cup dried hibiscus blossoms

2 cups Demerara Syrup (see page 256)

1. Place the hibiscus blossoms and syrup in a large mason jar and let the mixture steep at room temperature for 6 hours.

2. Strain the syrup and use immediately or store in the refrigerator, where it will keep for up to 6 months.

MAPLE & PECAN FALERNUM

2 cups toasted pecan pieces

4 cups water

1½ cups sugar

Zest of 1 orange

Zest of 2 limes

2 cinnamon sticks, smashed

10 whole cloves

10 allspice berries

3 star anise pods

¼ cup chopped, unpeeled fresh ginger

1 cup maple sugar

1 cup maple syrup

1 oz. orange juice

1 oz. fresh lime juice

Hamilton Guyana 151 rum, as needed

1. Divide the pecans between two large mason jars. Cover the pecans with the water and let the mixture steep for 24 hours.

2. Place the sugar in a large container. Add the orange zest and lime zest and muddle the mixture until it is an oleo saccharum (sugar oil). Let the oleo saccharum sit for 24 hours.

3. Place the cinnamon sticks, cloves, allspice, and star anise in a large saucepan and toast them over medium-high heat for 1 minute, shaking the pan frequently.

4. Add the pecan mixtures, oleo saccharum, and ginger and reduce the heat to medium. Bring the mixture to a simmer and cook for 30 minutes, taking care not to burn the sugar or let the mixture boil over.

5. Strain the syrup and place it in a clean saucepan. Warm the syrup over medium-low heat, add the maple sugar, maple syrup, orange juice, and lime juice, and stir until the sugar has dissolved. Cook until the maple flavor is to your liking.

6. Remove the pan from heat and let the mixture cool.

7. Strain the mixture into a large mason jar. Add 1 oz. rum for every 5 oz. of the mixture. Cover the jar, shake to combine, and use immediately or store at room temperature for up to 1 year.

YUZU SYRUP

2 oz. fresh yuzu juice

1 cup water

1 cup honey

1. Place all of the ingredients in a saucepan and bring the mixture to a boil over medium heat, stirring to combine.

2. Remove the pan from heat and let the syrup cool before using or storing in the refrigerator, where the syrup will keep for up to 1 month.

COCONUT RUM BLEND

1 cup Appleton Estate Signature Blend rum

1 cup Appleton Estate Reserve Blend rum

½ cup Smith & Cross rum

¼ cup coconut oil

1. Place the ingredients in a mason jar, seal it, and shake to combine. Let the mixture steep for 3 days.

2. Place the mason jar in the freezer and chill until the oil solidifies on top of the rum.

3. Remove the layer of solidified oil, strain the rum through a coffee filter, and use immediately or store at room temperature.

BLACK CURRANT–INFUSED RUM

1 cup black currants

1 (750 ml) bottle of Appleton Estate Reserve Blend rum

1. Place the currants and rum in a large mason jar and let the mixture steep for 3 days.

2. Strain the infused rum before using or storing at room temperature.

BANANA SYRUP

2 bananas, peeled and sliced

1 cup sugar

½ cup water

Pinch of fine sea salt

1. Place the bananas and sugar in a saucepan, stir until the bananas are coated, and let them macerate for 3 hours.

2. Add the water and salt and bring the mixture to a boil over medium heat, stirring to dissolve the sugar.

3. Remove the pan from heat and let the syrup cool. Strain the syrup before using or storing in the refrigerator, where the syrup will keep for up to 1 month.

TIKI MIX

1 cup pineapple juice

½ nutmeg seed, grated

½ oz. St. Elizabeth Allspice Dram

¼ oz. Angostura Bitters

1 large cinnamon stick

1. Place all of the ingredients in a blender and puree for 30 seconds.

2. Strain the mixture into a mason jar before using or storing in the refrigerator, where it will keep for up to 1 month.

SAGE & MINT AGAVE

9 oz. agave

2½ oz. water

50 fresh mint leaves

8 fresh sage leaves

1. Place all of the ingredients in a blender and puree until smooth.

2. Strain the mixture through a piece of cheesecloth before using or storing at room temperature.

PINK PEPPER & POMEGRANATE SYRUP

2 cups 100 percent pomegranate juice

2 tablespoons sugar

1 tablespoon fresh lemon juice

1 teaspoon pink peppercorns

1. Place the pomegranate juice in a saucepan and bring it to a boil.

2. Add the remaining ingredients, reduce the heat, and simmer the mixture for 30 minutes.

3. Remove the pan from heat and let the syrup cool.

4. Strain the syrup before using or storing in the refrigerator, where it will keep for up to 1 month.

HIBISCUS-INFUSED RUM

⅔ oz. dried hibiscus blossoms

4 cups Smith & Cross rum

1. Place the ingredients in a large mason jar and let the mixture steep for 48 hours.

2. Strain the infused rum before using or storing at room temperature.

VANILLA & CHILE SYRUP

1 cup water

2 cups demerara sugar

2 jalapeño chile peppers, chopped

4 vanilla beans

1. Place the water in a saucepan and bring it to a boil.

2. Add the demerara sugar and stir until it has dissolved.

3. Remove the pan from heat and stir in the jalapeños. Halve the vanilla beans, scrape the seeds into the syrup, and add the pods as well. Stir to combine and let the syrup cool completely.

4. Strain the syrup before using or storing in the refrigerator, where it will keep for up to 3 months.

HONEY SYRUP

1½ cups water

1½ cups honey

1. Place the water in a saucepan and bring it to a boil.

2. Add the honey and cook until it is just runny.

3. Remove the pan from heat and let the syrup cool before using or storing in the refrigerator, where it will keep for up to 1 month.

BROWN SUGAR SYRUP

1 cup water

2 cups brown sugar

1. Place the water in a saucepan and bring it to a boil.

2. Add the brown sugar and stir until it has dissolved.

3. Remove the pan from heat and let the syrup cool before using or storing in the refrigerator, where it will keep for up to 6 months.

SALINE SOLUTION

1 oz. salt

9 oz. water

1. Place the ingredients in a mason jar and stir until the salt has dissolved.

2. Use immediately or store at room temperature.

SIMPLE SYRUP

1 cup water

2 cups sugar

1. Place the water in a saucepan and bring it to a boil.

2. Add the sugar and stir until it has dissolved.

3. Remove the pan from heat and let the syrup cool before using or storing in the refrigerator, where it will keep for up to 3 months.

WATERMELON SHRUB

Juice from 1 pressed watermelon

2 cups apple cider vinegar

2 cups sugar

1. Place the watermelon juice and vinegar in a saucepan and bring the mixture to a simmer.

2. Add the sugar and stir until it has dissolved.

3. Remove the pan from heat and let the shrub cool before using or storing in the refrigerator, where it will keep for up to 6 months.

FERNET-BRANCA REDUCTION

½ cup Fernet-Branca

½ cup sugar

1. Place the Fernet-Branca in a saucepan and bring it to a simmer.

2. Add the sugar and stir until it has dissolved.

3. Remove the pan from heat and let the reduction cool before using or storing in the refrigerator, where it will keep for up to 6 months.

BLUE WRAY & NEPHEW

¾ cup Wray & Nephew rum

¼ cup blue curaçao

1. Place the ingredients in a mason jar and stir to combine.

2. Use immediately or store at room temperature.

PINEAPPLE SYRUP

1 pineapple, trimmed and cut into 1-inch cubes

4 cups sugar

1. Place the ingredients in a large container and let the pineapple macerate for 4 hours.

2. Place the mixture in a blender and puree until smooth.

3. Strain the syrup before using or storing in the refrigerator, where it will keep for up to 1 month.

PUMPKIN SYRUP

1 cup water

1 cup demerara sugar

1 cup pumpkin puree

1. Place the water in a saucepan and bring it to a boil.

2. Add the sugar and stir until it has dissolved.

3. Stir in the pumpkin puree and cook for 1 minute, stirring continually. Remove the pan from heat and let the syrup cool.

4. Strain the syrup before using or storing in the refrigerator, where it will keep for up to 1 month.

CITRIC ACID SOLUTION

35 oz. water

2 oz. citric acid

1. Place the ingredients in a large mason jar and stir until combined. Use immediately or store at room temperature.

GINGER SYRUP

1 cup water

1 cup sugar

2-inch piece of fresh ginger, unpeeled and chopped

1. Place the water in a saucepan and bring it to a boil.

2. Add the sugar and stir until it has dissolved.

3. Stir in the ginger, remove the pan from heat, and let the syrup cool.

4. Strain the syrup before using or storing in the refrigerator, where it will keep for up to 1 month.

PINEAPPLE-INFUSED SAILOR JERRY

1 (750 ml) bottle of Sailor Jerry rum

10½ oz. pineapple, chopped

1. Place the ingredients in a mason jar and let the mixture steep for 1 week.

2. Strain the infused rum before using or storing at room temperature.

RASPBERRY & POMEGRANATE SHRUB

10½ oz. 100 percent pomegranate juice

10 oz. caster (superfine) sugar

1½ oz. raspberry vinegar

1. Place all of the ingredients in a saucepan and warm the mixture over medium heat, stirring until the sugar has dissolved.

2. Remove the pan from heat and let the shrub cool before using or storing in the refrigerator.

SPICED RUM

6 whole cloves

1 cinnamon stick

6 allspice berries

10 black peppercorns

¼ cup Demerara Syrup
(see page 256)

2 (750 ml) bottles of Wray
& Nephew rum

1 vanilla bean

1. Place the cloves, cinnamon stick, allspice berries, and peppercorns in a saucepan and toast them over medium-low heat until they are fragrant, about 1 minute, shaking the pan occasionally.

2. Remove the pan from heat, add the syrup and 1 tablespoon of the rum, and stir to combine.

3. Split the vanilla bean in half, scrape the seeds into the rum mixture, and add the pod as well.

4. Add enough of the remaining rum that the mixture is easy to pour, pour it into a large mason jar, and then add the remaining rum.

5. Store the jar in a cool, dark place and let the mixture steep until the flavor is to your liking.

6. Strain the rum before using or storing at room temperature.

BLUE MARINER CURAÇAO

1 cup Grand Marnier

1 cup Demerara Syrup
(see page 256)

4 oz. Green Chartreuse

2 tablespoons blue food coloring

1. Place all of the ingredients in a large mason jar, cover it, and shake until combined.

2. Use immediately or store at room temperature.

CHAMOMILE SYRUP

1 cup water

2 cups sugar

5 bags of chamomile tea

1. Place the water in a saucepan and bring it to a boil.

2. Add the sugar and stir until it has dissolved.

3. Add the tea, remove the pan from heat, and let the syrup steep as it cools.

4. Strain the syrup before using or storing in the refrigerator, where it will keep for up to 1 month.

#9

2 oz. Real Ginger Syrup

1 oz. almond paste

1 teaspoon St. Elizabeth Allspice Dram

1. Place the ginger syrup and almond paste in a container and stir until combined.

2. Stir in the allspice dram and either use immediately or store in the refrigerator, where it will keep for up to 3 months.

PASSION FRUIT CORDIAL

17½ oz. passion fruit puree

3½ oz. fructose

7 oz. caster (superfine) sugar

1. Place all of the ingredients in a mason jar and stir until the fructose and sugar have dissolved.

2. Use immediately or store in the refrigerator, where it will keep for up to 1 month.

BURNT SUGAR SYRUP

---

1 cup brown sugar

1 cup boiling water

1. Place the brown sugar in a saucepan and cook over low heat, swirling the pan occasionally, until the sugar has melted.

2. Cook for another minute and remove the pan from heat.

3. Slowly stir in the boiling water. Return the pan to the stove and cook over medium heat for 2 minutes.

4. Remove the pan from heat and let the syrup cool before using or storing in the refrigerator, where it will keep for up to 1 month.

COFFEE SYRUP

---

1 cup water

2¼ oz. brewed espresso

Dash of cinnamon

Dash of chili powder

2 cups sugar

1. Place the water, espresso, cinnamon, and chili powder in a saucepan and bring the mixture to a boil, stirring occasionally.

2. Add the sugar and stir until it has dissolved.

3. Remove the pan from heat and let the syrup cool.

4. Strain the syrup before using or storing in the refrigerator, where it will keep for up to 1 month.

RED PEPPER SYRUP

9 oz. water

2 red bell peppers, stems and seeds removed, chopped

17½ oz. demerara sugar

1. Place the water in a saucepan and bring it to a boil.

2. Add the bell peppers and demerara sugar and stir until the sugar has dissolved.

3. Remove the pan from heat and let the syrup cool.

4. Pour the mixture, without straining, into a mason jar and chill it in the refrigerator overnight.

5. Strain the syrup before using or storing in the refrigerator, where it will keep for up to 1 month.

BROWN BUTTER–WASHED HANATARE

5⅓ oz. unsalted butter

1 (750 ml) bottle of hanatare brown sugar shōchū

1. Place the butter in a saucepan and melt it over medium heat.

2. Remove the pan from heat, add the shōchū, and gently stir to combine. Let the mixture steep for 2 hours.

3. Strain the washed shōchū through a coffee filter before using or storing in the refrigerator, where it will keep for up to 2 months.

SALTED PISTACHIO SYRUP

3½ oz. raw pistachio nuts

17½ oz. sugar

25⅓ oz. warm water

1 tablespoon fine sea salt

1. Place the pistachios in a dry skillet and toast them over medium heat until they start to brown, 6 to 8 minutes.

2. Place the toasted pistachios, sugar, water, and salt in a blender and puree until combined.

3. Strain before using or storing in the refrigerator, where it will keep for up to 1 month.

HERB TEA

2 tablespoons fresh rosemary

2 tablespoons fresh thyme

2 tablespoons fresh oregano

2 teaspoons freshly ground black pepper

2 cups boiling water

1. Place all of the ingredients in a mason jar, stir to combine, and let the mixture steep overnight.

2. Strain before using or storing at room temperature.

HIBISCUS TINCTURE

Dried hibiscus blossoms, as needed

2 cups pisco

1. Fill a pint mason jar to the top with dried hibiscus blossoms and then fill the jar with the pisco. Let the mixture steep overnight.

2. Strain the mixture before using or storing at room temperature.

PASSION FRUIT HONEY

1 cup honey

1 cup passion fruit puree

1. Place the honey in a saucepan and warm it over medium heat until it is runny.

2. Pour the honey into a mason jar, stir in the passion fruit puree, and let the mixture cool before using or storing in the refrigerator, where it will keep for up to 1 month.

PAPAYA SHRUB

1 cup papaya nectar

2 cups apple cider vinegar

2 cups sugar

1. Place the papaya nectar and vinegar in a saucepan and bring the mixture to a simmer.

2. Add the sugar and stir until it has dissolved.

3. Remove the pan from heat and let the shrub cool before using or storing in the refrigerator, where it will keep for up to 6 months.

THAI CHILI TINCTURE

4 bird's eye chili peppers, stems and seeds removed, chopped

1 (750 ml) bottle of Wray & Nephew rum

1. Place the ingredients in a large mason jar and let the mixture steep for 2 weeks.

2. Strain the tincture before using or storing at room temperature.

PEAR & CARDAMOM HORCHATA

3½ cinnamon sticks

14 green cardamom pods

¾ nutmeg seed

7 cups pear juice

4 cups water

4¼ cups jasmine rice

1 lb. honey

1 vanilla bean

Zest of 1 lime

Cinnamon Syrup
(see page 260), as needed

1. Preheat the oven to 350°F. Place the cinnamon sticks, cardamom pods, and nutmeg seed on a baking sheet, place it in the oven, and toast the spices for 20 minutes. Remove them from the oven and let them cool.

2. Place the pear juice, water, rice, honey, vanilla bean, lime zest, and toasted aromatics in a large container and let the mixture steep at room temperature overnight.

3. Working in batches, place the mixture in a food processor and blitz until smooth. Double-strain the mixture, pressing down on the solids to extract as much liquid as possible.

4. For every 4 cups of horchata, stir in 2 oz. of Cinnamon Syrup. Use immediately or store in the refrigerator, where the horchata will keep for up to 1 week.

COCONUT BUTTER–WASHED PISCO

14 oz. coconut oil

1 (750 ml) bottle of pisco

1. Place the coconut oil in a saucepan and melt it over medium heat.

2. Pour the coconut oil into a mason jar, add the pisco, and stir to combine. Let the mixture steep at room temperature overnight.

3. Remove the layer of solidified oil. Strain the pisco through a coffee filter before using or storing at room temperature.

SUGAR SNAP PEA SYRUP

4 oz. water

1 lb. sugar

5⅓ oz. fresh sugar snap pea juice (from about 2 lbs. sugar snap peas)

1. Place the water in a saucepan and bring it to a boil.

2. Add the sugar and stir until it has dissolved. Remove the pan from heat and let the syrup cool.

3. Stir in the sugar snap pea juice and use immediately or store in the refrigerator, where the syrup will keep for up to 1 week.

Metric Conversions

US Measurement	Approximate Metric Liquid Measurement	Approximate Metric Dry Measurement
1 teaspoon	5 ml	5 g
1 tablespoon or ½ ounce	15 ml	14 g
1 ounce or ⅛ cup	30 ml	29 g
¼ cup or 2 ounces	60 ml	57 g
⅓ cup	80 ml	76 g
½ cup or 4 ounces	120 ml	113 g
⅔ cup	160 ml	151 g
¾ cup or 6 ounces	180 ml	170 g
1 cup or 8 ounces or ½ pint	240 ml	227 g
1½ cups or 12 ounces	350 ml	340 g
2 cups or 1 pint or 16 ounces	475 ml	454 g
3 cups or 1½ pints	700 ml	680 g
4 cups or 2 pints or 1 quart	950 ml	908 g

Index

ABOUT CIDER MILL PRESS
BOOK PUBLISHERS

Good ideas ripen with time. From seed to harvest, Cider Mill Press brings fine reading, information, and entertainment together between the covers of its creatively crafted books. Our Cider Mill bears fruit twice a year, publishing a new crop of titles each spring and fall.

CIDER MILL
PRESS

BOOK
PUBLISHERS

"Where Good Books Are Ready for Press"

Visit us online at
cidermillpress.com

or write to us at
PO Box 454
12 Spring St.
Kennebunkport, Maine 04046